SPANISH PICTURE DICTIONARY

SANTILLANA USA

SANTILLANA USA
Language Education Experts

Spanish Picture Dictionary
© 2012 Santillana USA Publishing Company, Inc.

Published in the United States of America.

Syllabus and Text: **Mizar Multimedia**

Editorial Directors: **Aurora Martín de Santa Olalla**
Developmental Editors: **Mercedes Fontecha, Susana Gómez, M.ª Antonia Oliva**

Linguistic and Cultural Advisors in Latin America and the United States: **Jorge Arriola, Luisa Helen Frey** († 2009) (Centro de Enseñanza de Lenguas Extranjeras [CELE], UNAM), **Isabel Mendoza** (Santillana USA)

Art Direction: **José Crespo**

Inside Pages: **Mizar Multimedia**
Illustrator: **Jorge Arranz**

Project Director: **Rosa Marín**
Picture Coordinator: **Carlos Aguilera**
Project Development Director: **Javier Tejeda**
Graphic Development: **Raúl de Andrés, José Luis García**

Production Manager: **Ángel García Encinar**

Production Coordinator: **Marisa Valbuena**
Layout: **Javier Pulido**

Translators: **Mizar Multimedia, Jacqueline Cook**
Proofreaders: **Gerardo Z. García, Liz Pease, Enrique Saulle**

ISBN: 978-1-61435-948-7

Santillana USA Publishing Company, Inc. 2023 NW 84th Avenue, Doral, FL 33122
www.prisaediciones.com

PRISA EDICIONES

Printed in USA by NuPress of Miami
15 14 13 12   1 2 3 4 5 6 7 8 9 10

Spanish Picture Dictionary

The Spanish Picture Dictionary, which aims to teach and reinforce vocabulary, is designed for adult and young adult students studying Spanish as a second or foreign language. It can be used as a complement to Spanish classes or as material for self-learning.

The dictionary contains more than 1,300 elementary-level items (nouns, adjectives, verbs, and expressions) in Spanish. The words are grouped into 24 thematically linked units and are related to the most common situations and needs that an adult student may have, from the most basic (food, clothes, and family) to the very specific (bank, post office, cars, and the road).

For the practice and consolidation of the vocabulary presented, enjoyable activities (fill-in-the blanks, word scrambles, crosswords and word searches) are included with their respective answers.

In addition, the dictionary offers an introduction to Spanish pronunciation with examples extracted from the vocabulary presented.

Lastly, the book includes two glossaries: Spanish-English and English-Spanish with cross-references to the unit and page numbers where the term can be found.

How to use this dictionary

Scenes

The vocabulary in each unit is presented on a two-page spread. On the left-hand page there is a full scene where the words to be presented are numbered. On the right-hand page more words are presented based on detailed illustrations from this scene. The words are always listed, one way or another, with their English translation.

At the end of the two-page presentation, some short dialogues and expressions related to the situations in the unit are included.

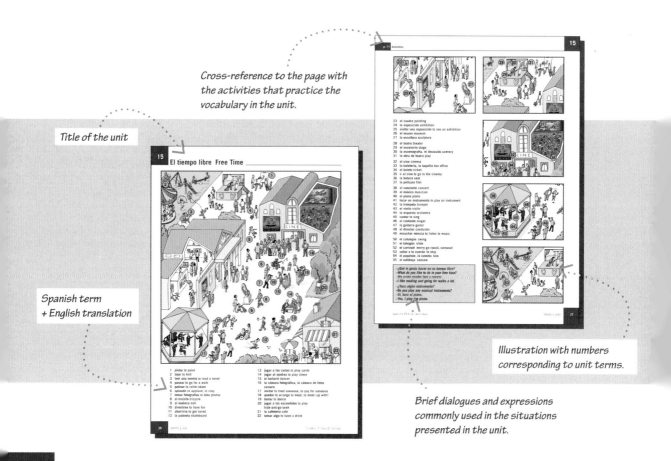

Cross-reference to the page with the activities that practice the vocabulary in the unit.

Title of the unit

Spanish term + English translation

Illustration with numbers corresponding to unit terms.

Brief dialogues and expressions commonly used in the situations presented in the unit.

Activities

The purpose of the activities is to practice and consolidate the vocabulary presented in each unit. Fill-in-the blanks, word scrambles, crosswords, and word searches are just some of the enjoyable activities that are included, all with their respective answers.

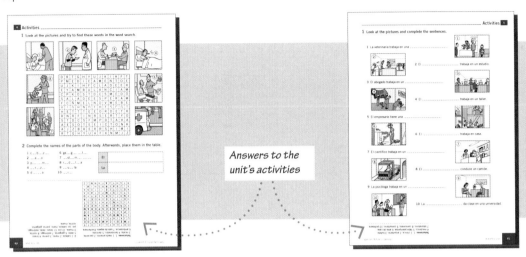

Answers to the unit's activities

Glossaries

The alphabetic lists of the words presented in the dictionary help the student to find them quickly.

Spanish-English

English-Spanish

Cross-reference to the unit and page where the word is presented.

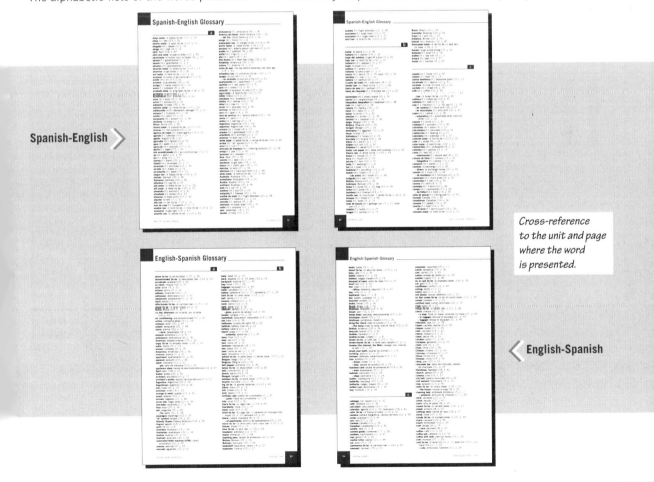

The pronunciation of Spanish

The pronunciation of Spanish is generally quite clear from its spelling. This feature makes Spanish a very easy language to pronounce.

The following set of guidelines should be sufficient for an English speaker to understand what written Spanish sounds like.

Also, remember that Spanish is spoken in many countries, so there is a good chance that some sounds will be slightly different from country to country, just like some sounds are different in the United States than they are in Great Britain.

Vowels

The sound system for vowels in Spanish is somewhat simpler than the English system. They are short and clearly pronunced, and unlike in English, are not extended to form a combination of two sounds. For example, the English word **no** sounds like *nou* with a **u** sound at the end. In contrast, the Spanish **no** has only the **o** sound without the **u** sound.

Spanish has only five vowels: **a**, **e**, **i**, **o** and **u**. This contrasts with English where vowels have different sounds depending on the sounds before and after the vowel.

a la a	Similar to 'f**a**ther.'	Am**é**ri**ca**
e la e	Similar to 'b**e**d.'	j**e**f**e**
i la i	Similar to 's**ee**d.'	d**í**a
o la o	Similar to 'c**o**ld.'	h**o**ra
u la u	Similar to 'm**oo**n.'	c**u**mpleaños
	Silent after **q** and in the groups **gue**, **gui**, unless marked by two dots over the **u** (ping**ü**ino).	q**u**erer, jug**u**etería, g**u**itarra

Diphthongs

Many Spanish diphthongs (the combination of two vowels pronounced in the same syllable) are similar to uses in English.

ai, ay	Similar to 's**i**de.'	b**ai**lar
au	Similar to 's**ou**nd.'	**Au**stralia
ei, ey	Similar to 'th**ey**.'	p**ei**ne
eu	Similar to '**may you**', without the sound of the **y**.	**Eu**ropa
oi, oy	Similar to 'b**oy**.'	s**oy**

Consonants

b la be	Similar to '**b**oat.'	**b**arco
c la ce	Similar to '**c**at' when followed by **a**, **o**, or **u**.	**c**ama, **c**omer, **c**uchara
	Similar to '**s**igh' when followed by **e** or **i**.	**c**ena
	In Spain, similar to '**th**anks' when followed by **e** or **i**.	**c**ena
ch la che	Similar to 'mu**ch**.'	cu**ch**illo
d la de	Similar to '**d**oor.'	**d**iente
f la efe	Similar to '**f**ake.'	so**f**á
g la ge	Similar to '**g**o' when followed by **a**, **o**, or **u**. Similar to '**g**uest' and '**g**uilty' in the group **gue**, **gui**. Note that the **u** is silent except when marked by two dots over the **u** (**ü**).	**g**ato, ami**g**o, yo**g**ur, man**g**uera, **g**uisante, nicara**g**üense
	Similar to '**h**ello' when followed by **e** or **i**. Note that this sound is harder in Spain than in Latin America.	**g**el, **g**imnasio
h la hache	Always silent (don't pronounce it at all).	**h**otel
j la jota	Similar to '**h**ello.' Note that **je** sounds like **ge**, and **ji** sounds like **gi**.	**j**amón, mu**j**er, **j**irafa
k la ka	Similar to 'fa**k**e.'	**k**ilo

l la ele	Similar to 'letter.'	lámpara
ll la elle	Similar to 'jail.'	apellido
m la eme	Similar to 'mom.'	mamá
n la ene	Similar to 'never.'	noche
ñ la eñe	Similar to 'cognac.'	mañana
p la pe	Similar to 'Napa.'	papá
q la cu	Similar to 'kilo.' Note that it is always followed by **ue** or **ui** and the **u** is silent.	queso, equipo
r la ere	Similar to 'butter.' Similar to 'rolling' at the beginning of a word and also after **l**, **n**, or **s**.	hora rojo, Israel
rr la erre	Similar to 'rolling.'	arroz
s la ese	Similar to 'seat.'	sábado
t la te	Similar to 'pass**ed**.'	moto
v la uve, la ve, la ve baja, la ve chica, la ve corta	Similar to 'boy.' Note that **v** sounds like **b**.	vaca
w la uve doble, la ve doble, la doble ve, la doble u	Similar to 'boy' in foreign words which have been incorporated into Spanish. Pronounced as **u** or as **gu** in foreign words which have not yet been adapted to Spanish.	Kuwait kiwi
x la equis	Similar to 'box.' Similar to 'hotel' in certain words. Note that this sound is harder in Spain than in Latin America.	taxi México
y la i griega	Similar to 'seed' when uses as a vowel, in the conjunction **y**, as well as at the end of words. Note that it is pronounced like **i**. Similar to 'jail.' Note that **y** sounds like **ll**.	y, hoy desayunar
z la zeta	Similar to 'sigh.' In Spain, similar to 'thanks.' In Spain, note that **za**, **zo**, **zu** sound like **ce**, **ci**.	zapato zapato

Placing the stress

There are simple rules for placing stress on Spanish words:

1. If a word ends in a vowel, or in **n** or **s** (most Spanish words), the second to last syllable is stressed: **ca**sa, **jo**ven, pa**ta**ta.
2. If the word ends in a consonant other than **n** or **s**, the last syllable is stressed: mu**jer**, re**loj**, alba**ñil**.
3. If the word needs to be stressed in some way contrary to rules 1 and 2, a written accent (also called **tilde**) is written over the vowel to be stressed: Pana**má**, ca**mión**, fran**cés**, me**cá**nico, **lá**piz.

Remember that monosyllables do not have written accents, unless they need to be distinguished from another monosyllable that means something different: **tú** ('you')/**tu** ('your').

La familia The Family

1	ser divorciado, estar divorciado to be divorced
2	el hijo único only child
3	la esposa wife
4	el esposo husband
5	ser viudo, estar viudo to be widowed
6	los gemelos, los mellizos twins
7	ser casado, estar casado to be married
8	la boda wedding
9	ser soltero, estar soltero to be single
10	la nuera daughter-in-law
11	la tía aunt
12	el tío uncle
13	la sobrina niece
14	el yerno son-in-law
15	el sobrino nephew
16	la suegra mother-in-law
17	el cuñado brother-in-law
18	el novio boyfriend
19	la novia girlfriend
20	el amigo friend
21	la fiesta de cumpleaños birthday party
22	la vela candle
23	el pastel de cumpleaños birthday cake
24	el regalo gift

25 acostarse to go to bed
26 dormir to sleep
27 bañarse to take a bath
28 afeitarse to shave
29 hablar to talk
30 ducharse to take a shower
31 lavarse los dientes to brush one's teeth
32 levantarse to get up
33 lavarse las manos to wash one's hands
34 peinarse to comb one's hair

35 leer el periódico to read the newspaper
36 ver la televisión to watch TV
37 vestirse to get dressed

38 los padres parents
39 el padre, el papá father
40 la madre, la mamá mother
41 el hijo son
42 la hija daughter
43 el hermano brother
44 la hermana sister
45 la prima cousin
46 el primo cousin
47 el abuelo grandfather
48 los abuelos grandparents
49 el nieto grandson
50 la nieta granddaughter
51 la abuela grandmother

—¿Está casado?
—Are you married?
—No, estoy divorciado.
—No, I'm divorced.

—¿Tiene hermanos?
—Do you have any brothers or sisters?

—Sí, tengo dos hermanas y un hermano.
—Yes, I have two sisters and a brother.
—Yo soy hijo único.
—I'm an only child.

—¡Feliz cumpleaños!
—Happy Birthday!

La descripción física Physical Descriptions _____

1 el niño child, boy
2 el adolescente adolescent, teenager
3 el anciano, el viejito elderly person, old man
4 el adulto adult
5 estar embarazada to be pregnant
6 el bebé baby
7 persona con discapacidad física physically challenged
8 estar ciego, persona con discapacidad visual to be blind, sight impaired
9 la mujer woman
10 el hombre man

11 ser alto to be tall
12 ser bajo to be short
13 ser guapo to be good-looking
14 parecerse a alguien to look like someone
15 estar sordo, persona con discapacidad auditiva to be deaf, hearing impaired
16 tener buena figura to have a good figure
17 ser gordo to be fat
18 ser delgado to be thin
19 ser fuerte to be strong
20 ser joven to be young
21 ser mayor, ser viejo to be older, to be old

22 llevar fleco, llevar flequillo to have bangs
23 tener un lunar to have a mole, to have a beauty mark
24 estar calvo to be bald

25 tener pelo rubio, ser rubio to be blond
26 estar bronceado to be tan, to have dark skin
27 tener pelo negro to be dark-haired
28 tener pelo castaño to be brown-haired, to have brown hair
29 tener el pelo canoso to have white hair
30 tener canas to have gray hair
31 tener el pelo corto to have short hair
32 tener trenzas to have braids
33 tener el pelo largo to have long hair
34 tener el pelo rizado to have curly hair
35 tener pecas to have freckles
36 ser pelirrojo to be red-haired, to have red hair
37 tener el pelo liso to have straight hair
38 tener colitas to have a ponytail

39 tener los ojos pequeños to have small eyes
40 tener los ojos grandes to have big eyes
41 tener los ojos azules to have blue eyes
42 tener ojos claros to have light-colored eyes
43 tener los ojos de color café, tener los ojos marrones to have brown eyes
44 tener los ojos verdes to have green eyes
45 tener ojos oscuros to have dark eyes
46 tener los ojos negros to have black eyes

47 tener bigote to have a mustache
48 tener barba to have a beard
49 tener puesta una gorra to wear a cap
50 usar lentes, usar gafas to wear glasses

–¿Quién es ese chico que usa lentes?
–Who's that guy wearing glasses?
–Es mi amigo Rodrigo.
–He's my friend Rodrigo.

–¿Cuántos años tiene?
–How old are you?
–Tengo treinta y cuatro años.
–I'm thirty-four years old.

–¿Cómo es su papá?
–What does your father look like?
–Es alto y moreno. Tiene los ojos verdes y barba.
Yo me parezco mucho a él.
–He's tall and dark. He has green eyes and a beard.
I look a lot like him.

–¡Qué chico más guapo!
–What a good-looking guy!

–¿Cuánto mide?
–How tall are you?
–1,80 (1 metro y 80 centímetros).
–One meter 80.

–¿Cuánto pesa?
–How much do you weigh?
–65 kilos.
–65 kilos.

25,4 milímetros (mm) = 1 pulgada
25.4 milimeters (mm) = 1 inch

0,3048 metros (m) = 1 pie
0.3048 meters (m) = 1 foot

453,59237 gramos (g) = 1 libra
453.59237 grams (g) = 1 pound

1 ser inteligente to be intelligent
2 ser flojo, ser vago to be lazy
3 ser obediente to be obedient
4 ser gracioso to be funny
5 ser trabajador to be hardworking
6 ser optimista to be optimistic
7 ser simpático to be friendly
8 ser pesimista to be pessimistic
9 ser travieso to be mischievous
10 estar nervioso to be nervous
11 estar tranquilo to be calm

12 ser serio to be serious
13 estar contento to be happy
14 ser alegre to be happy
15 ser egoísta to be selfish
16 ser antipático to be unfriendly
17 ser tímido to be shy
18 estar preocupado to be worried
19 estar triste to be sad
20 ser sociable to be sociable
21 ser amable to be kind, to be nice
22 ser generoso to be generous

23 tener frío to be cold
24 ser despistado to be absentminded
25 tener sueño to be sleepy, to be tired

26 estar aburrido to be bored
27 tener sed to be thirsty
28 ser desordenado to be messy

29 ser impaciente to be impatient
30 tener hambre to be hungry
31 ser ordenado to be neat

–¿Qué le pasa?
–What's wrong?, What's the matter?
–Estoy un poco triste. Extraño
mucho a mis papás.
–I'm a little sad. I miss my parents
a lot.

–¡Te quiero!
–I love you!

–Me dan mucho asco las arañas.
–Spiders are really disgusting.

–Marta y yo nos llevamos muy bien.
–Marta and I get along really well.

32 tener calor to be hot
33 estar enojado to be angry
34 estar cansado to be tired
35 reir to laugh
36 ser cariñoso to be
    affectionate
37 querer to love
38 besar to kiss
39 gustar to like
40 dar vergüenza to be
    embarrassed
41 llorar to cry
42 dar asco to disgust,
    to gross out
43 tener miedo to be afraid

44 odiar to hate
45 estar orgulloso to be proud
46 ser educado to be polite,
    to be well-mannered
47 estar lleno to be full
48 estar enamorado to be in love
49 extrañar, echar de menos
    to miss
50 ser maleducado to be rude,
    to be ill-mannered
51 estar sorprendido to be
    surprised
52 ser hablador to be talkative
53 ser envidioso to be envious,
    to be jealous

La ropa Clothes

1 el probador fitting room
2 estar largo to be long
3 estar corto to be short
4 la talla size
5 el gancho, la percha hanger
6 ser feo to be ugly
7 ser lindo, ser bonito to be nice, to be pretty
8 desabrocharse to unbutton, to unfasten
9 estar ancho to be loose
10 la corbata tie

11 ser a rayas to be striped
12 ser liso to be plain
13 ser a lunares to be polka-dotted
14 el cinturón belt
15 ponerse to put on
16 quitarse to take off
17 el paraguas umbrella
18 estar estrecho to be tight
19 abrocharse to button (up), to fasten
20 probarse to try on

21 los (pantalones) vaqueros,
   jeans jeans
22 la blusa blouse
23 la falda skirt
24 el vestido dress
25 el suéter sweater

26 el abrigo coat
27 la camisa shirt
28 el pantalón, los pantalones
   pants
29 la chaqueta jacket
30 el traje suit
31 el saco jacket

32 las botas boots
33 los zapatos shoes
34 los zapatos de tacón
   high-heeled shoes
35 las pantuflas slippers
36 las sandalias sandals
37 los calcetines socks
38 las medias stockings

39 el sujetador, el sostén bra
40 los calzones, las bragas panties
41 los calzoncillos underpants
42 el/la pijama, el/la piyama pajamas
43 el traje de baño swimsuit
44 el bikini bikini

45 los lentes de sol, las gafas
   de sol sunglasses
46 los guantes gloves
47 la bufanda scarf
48 la bolsa, el bolso purse
49 el reloj watch
50 el collar necklace

51 los aretes earrings
52 el sombrero hat
53 la sortija, el anillo
   ring
54 la pulsera bracelet
55 la pañoleta, el pañuelo
   scarf

–¿Puedo probarme este suéter?
–Can I try this sweater on?

–¿Cómo le quedan los pantalones?
–How do the pants fit?
–Me quedan un poco largos.
–They're a bit long.

–Perdone, ¿tiene la talla mediana?
–Excuse me, do you have this in a medium?

–¡Qué vestido tan bonito! Me gusta mucho.
–What a pretty dress! I really like it.

Las profesiones Jobs

1. **el vendedor** sales representative
2. **el camionero** truck driver
3. **el funcionario** civil servant
4. **el alcalde** mayor
5. **el intérprete** translator, interpreter
6. **el sacerdote** priest
7. **el abogado** lawyer
8. **el juez** judge
9. **el periodista** journalist
10. **el fotógrafo** photographer
11. **ser licenciado** to have a degree, to be college graduate
12. **el soldado** soldier
13. **el actor** actor
14. **la actriz** actress
15. **el ingeniero** engineer
16. **el jardinero** gardener
17. **el agricultor** farmer
18. **estar desempleado** to be unemployed
19. **estar jubilado** to be retired
20. **el chofer** bus driver
21. **el barrendero** street cleaner

22 el bufete law firm
23 el arquitecto architect
24 el estudio de arquitectura
    architect's studio
25 el psicólogo psychologist
26 el consultorio, la consulta
    del psicólogo
    psychologist's office
27 el veterinario veterinarian, vet
28 la clínica veterinaria
    veterinary clinic

29 el laboratorio laboratory,
    lab
30 el científico
    scientist
31 el estudiante student
32 la universidad
    university
33 el profesor teacher,
    professor
34 estudiar to study

35 el ejecutivo executive
36 el técnico en informática
    computer technician
37 el taller workshop
38 el mecánico mechanic
39 tener una empresa to have a
    business
40 el empresario business man
41 trabajar en una fábrica to work
    in a factory
42 la fábrica factory

43 el ama de casa housewife
44 el electricista electrician
45 el plomero
    plumber
46 el escritor writer
47 la empleada doméstica cleaning
    lady, domestic worker
48 el pintor painter
49 el albañil bricklayer
50 el carpintero carpenter

–¿A qué se dedica?
–What do you do?
–Soy maestra.
–I'm a teacher.

–¿Qué ha estudiado?
–What did you study?
–Soy licenciado en Ciencias Económicas y Empresariales.
–I have a degree in Economics and Business Studies.

1 el hospital hospital
2 tener fiebre to have a fever
3 el termómetro thermometer
4 estar enfermo to be sick
5 el medicamento medicine
6 el enfermero nurse
7 doler la cabeza to have a headache
8 la jeringa, la jeringuilla syringe
9 estar enyesado to be in a cast
10 el dentista dentist
11 la receta prescription
12 la radiografía X-ray

13 la ambulancia ambulance
14 toser to cough
15 tener gripa, tener gripe to have the flu
16 el médico doctor
17 el paciente patient
18 devolver, vomitar to throw up, to vomit
19 la sala de urgencias emergency room
20 estornudar to sneeze
21 tener un resfriado to have a cold, to be congested
22 el cirujano surgeon
23 la sala de espera waiting room

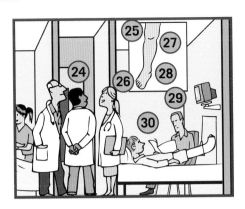

24 estar de pie to be standing
25 la pierna leg
26 el pie foot
27 la rodilla knee
28 el tobillo ankle
29 estar sentado to be sitting, to be seated
30 estar acostado to be lying down

31 la espalda back
32 el estómago stomach
33 el hombro shoulder
34 el pecho chest
35 el trasero, las nalgas bottom, buttocks

36 el brazo arm
37 el codo elbow
38 la muñeca wrist
39 la mano hand
40 el dedo pulgar thumb
41 el dedo índice index finger
42 el dedo corazón middle finger
43 el dedo anular ring finger
44 el dedo meñique little finger

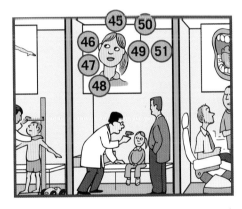

45 la cabeza head
46 la frente forehead
47 el cachete, la mejilla cheek
48 el cuello neck
49 la nariz nose
50 la oreja ear
51 el oído ear

52 la boca mouth
53 la muela molar
54 el diente tooth
55 los labios lips
56 la garganta throat
57 la lengua tongue

58 el ojo eye
59 las cejas eyebrows
60 la pupila pupil
61 las pestañas eyelashes
62 el párpado eyelid

–*¿Cómo está?*
–*How are you?*
–*Me encuentro mal.*
–*I don't feel well.*

–*¿Qué le pasa?*
–*What's wrong?, What's the matter?*
–*Me duele mucho la cabeza y tengo fiebre.*
–*My head hurts a lot and I have a fever.*

–*Soy diabético y soy alérgico a la penicilina.*
–*I'm diabetic and I'm allergic to penicillin.*

–*Tiene diarrea y se ha desmayado. Le vamos a hacer unos análisis.*
–*He has diarrhea and he fainted. We're going to do some tests on him.*

–*¡Achís!*
–*Achoo!*
–*¡Salud!*
–*Bless you!*

–*¡Que se mejore!*
–*Feel better!*

La vivienda The Apartment Building

1 el edificio building
2 el *penthouse* penthouse
3 el apartamento apartment
4 el tercer piso fourth floor
5 el segundo piso third floor
6 el estudio studio apartment
7 el primer piso second floor
8 la planta baja first floor, ground floor
9 estar adentro to be inside
10 estar afuera to be outside
11 estar debajo to be under
12 estar encima to be on top of
13 estar arriba to be above, to be on top of

14 estar lejos to be far
15 estar allá, estar allí to be over there, to be there
16 estar atrás, estar detrás to be behind
17 estar en el centro to be in the middle, to be in the center
18 estar entre to be between
19 estar abajo to be below
20 estar delante to be in front of
21 estar enfrente to be in front of
22 estar acá, estar aquí to be here
23 estar cerca to be near
24 estar al lado to be next to
25 la casa house

26 la escalera stairway
27 estar cerrado to be closed
28 estar abierto to be open
29 la terraza terrace
30 el techo ceiling
31 el aire acondicionado air
    conditioning
32 la pared wall
33 la calefacción heating
34 el elevador, el ascensor elevator
35 el timbre doorbell
36 la puerta door
37 el piso floor
38 la persiana blind
39 la ventana window
40 el pasillo hallway
41 el vecino neighbor
42 el portero doorman
43 el bote de basura, el contenedor
    de basura garbage can
44 mudarse to move
45 alquilar to rent

46 la antena antenna
47 la chimenea chimney
48 el techo, el tejado roof
49 vender to sell
50 el garaje garage
51 el jardín yard

–¿Dónde vive?
–Where do you live?
–En la calle Cervantes, número 29, 4.º B.
–At 29 Cervantes Street, 4th floor, Apt. B.

–Se vende o se alquila. Es un apartamento amplio y luminoso, con
aire acondicionado. Tiene dos habitaciones y dos baños. El precio
incluye un lugar para estacionar y un cuarto de los trastos.
–For sale or for rent. Spacious apartment with plenty of light and
air conditioning. There are two bedrooms and two bathrooms.
Price includes a parking space and storage space.

La casa The House

1	tender la cama to make the bed
2	la habitación bedroom
3	el (cuarto de) baño bathroom
4	el despacho office
5	limpiar la casa to clean the house
6	el comedor dining room
7	la sala, el salón living room
8	el recibidor entrance hall
9	el perchero coat rack
10	el espejo mirror
11	la cocina kitchen
12	estar sucio to be dirty
13	estar limpio to be clean
14	lavar los platos to wash the dishes
15	el enchufe socket
16	lavar en la lavadora to do a load of laundry

17 el reloj de pared clock
18 el librero, la estantería bookshelf
19 el televisor television
20 el (reproductor de) DVD DVD (player)
21 la alfombra rug
22 el sillón armchair
23 la lámpara lamp
24 el sofá sofa, couch
25 la silla chair
26 la vitrina glass cabinet
27 la mesa table
28 las cortinas curtains

29 el refrigerador, la nevera refrigerator
30 el microondas microwave
31 la estufa, la cocina electric stove
32 el lavaplatos dishwasher
33 la llave, el grifo faucet
34 el fregadero sink
35 el horno oven
36 la plancha iron
37 la lavadora washing machine

38 el armario closet
39 la mesita de noche nightstand
40 el despertador alarm clock
41 el edredón comforter
42 la cama matrimonial double bed
43 la lámpara desk lamp
44 la almohada pillow
45 las sábanas sheets
46 la cama bed
47 el escritorio desk
48 el jabón soap
49 el papel higiénico toilet paper
50 la pasta de dientes toothpaste
51 el cepillo de dientes toothbrush
52 el secador hair dryer
53 el champú shampoo
54 la ducha shower
55 el gel liquid soap, shower gel
56 la bañera, la tina bathtub
57 la esponja sponge
58 el peine, la peinilla comb
59 el lavabo, el lavamanos sink
60 la toalla towel
61 el inodoro toilet bowl, toilet

La ciudad The City

1	el barrio neighborhood	13	la escuela school
2	el edificio de apartamentos apartment building	14	seguir derecho, seguir recto to go straight
3	el parque park		
4	la biblioteca library	15	la esquina corner
5	salir to go out, to leave	16	la calle street
6	la avenida avenue	17	dar vuelta a la derecha, girar a la derecha to turn right
7	la plaza square		
8	el centro (de la ciudad) downtown	18	la iglesia church
9	el palacio municipal city hall	19	la acera sidewalk
10	las afueras the outskirts	20	entrar to come in, to go in
11	el rascacielos skyscraper	21	dar vuelta a la izquierda, girar a la izquierda to turn left
12	la cuadra, la manzana block		

22 la estación de tren train station
23 el tren train
24 tomar el tren to take the train
25 el andén platform

26 ir caminando, ir andando to walk
27 la parada de taxis taxi stand
28 el taxista taxi driver
29 el taxi taxi
30 ir en auto to go by car
31 el auto car
32 la moto motorcycle

33 el semáforo traffic light
34 el cruce peatonal crosswalk
35 cruzar la calle to cross
36 el peatón pedestrian
37 el autobús bus
38 la parada de autobús
   bus stop
39 bajar del autobús to get off a bus
40 subir al autobús to get on a bus

41 el estacionamiento parking lot
42 la cabina telefónica telephone booth
43 el farol, la farola streetlight
44 la fuente fountain
45 preguntar to ask
46 el bote de basura trash can
47 tirar al bote de basura
   to throw in the trash can
48 contestar to answer
49 el buzón mailbox
50 el banco bench
51 la estación de metro subway station
52 la alcantarilla sewer

–Perdone, ¿sabe dónde está la calle Almirante?
–Excuse me, do you know where Almirante Street is?

–Sí, está muy cerca. Cruce la plaza y después
tome la primera calle a la derecha. Esa es la calle
Almirante.
–Yes, you're very close. Cross the square and then take
the first street on your right. That's Almirante Street.

–Perdone, ¿sabe si hay una biblioteca por aquí cerca?
–Excuse me, do you know if there's a library near here?

–Sí, hay una al otro lado de la plaza.
–Yes, there's one on the other side of the square.

De compras Shopping

1 el centro comercial shopping center, shopping mall
2 devolver to return
3 el directorio directory
4 el precio price
5 las ofertas, las rebajas sales
6 el escaparate window display
7 cambiar to exchange
8 las escaleras eléctricas, las escaleras mecánicas escalator
9 la etiqueta tag
10 el ticket, el recibo receipt
11 el vendedor clerk
12 el cliente customer
13 comprar to buy
14 la salida de emergencia emergency exit
15 la bolsa bag
16 ir de compras to go shopping

17 la farmacia pharmacy
18 el farmacéutico pharmacist
19 la florería, la floristería florist
20 el ramo de rosas bouquet of roses
21 la flor flower
22 la planta plant
23 estar de oferta to be on sale
24 estar lleno to be full
25 estar vacío to be empty
26 la salida exit
27 la entrada entrance
28 la tintorería drycleaners
29 la óptica optician

30 la lavandería laundromat
31 el puesto de periódicos,
    el quiosco newspaper kiosk
32 la pastelería bakery
33 la tienda de electrodomésticos
    appliance store
34 la papelería stationery store
35 la heladería ice cream parlor
36 la librería bookstore
37 la perfumería drug store
38 la tienda de ropa clothing store
39 la juguetería toy store
40 la agencia de viajes travel agency

41 la tienda de discos record store
42 la peluquería hair salon
43 el peluquero hairdresser
44 la zapatería shoe store
45 la joyería jewelry store

—Quisiera un ramo de rosas, por favor.
—I'd like a bouquet of roses, please.

—Perdone, ¿cuánto cuestan estos zapatos?
—Excuse me, how much are these shoes?

El supermercado Supermarket

1 cortar to cut
2 la lista del supermercado, la lista de la compra shopping list
3 los congelados frozen foods
4 ir al supermercado, hacer la compra to go shopping
5 pagar en efectivo to pay (in) cash
6 pagar con tarjeta to pay with a credit card
7 hacer cola to wait in line
8 el cajero cashier
9 la caja checkout

10 las bebidas drinks
11 pesar to weigh
12 pedir to ask for
13 ser barato to be cheap
14 ser caro to be expensive
15 costar to cost
16 las conservas canned goods
17 los artículos de limpieza cleaning products
18 el carro shopping cart

19 la leche milk
20 el litro liter
21 el yogur yogurt
22 la frutería fruit chop
23 la fruta fruit
24 la verdura vegetables
25 el frutero fruit seller
26 el kilo kilo

27 los embutidos, los fiambres cold cuts
28 el jamón ham
29 el queso cheese
30 la carnicería butcher shop
31 el carnicero butcher
32 la carne meat
33 el cerdo pork
34 el pollo chicken
35 la carne de res beef

36 el pescado fish
37 la pescadería fish market
38 el pescadero fishmonger
39 el marisco shellfish

40 la botella bottle
41 la pasta pasta
42 el arroz rice
43 la harina flour
44 el paquete package
45 la lata can
46 la docena de huevos a dozen eggs
47 el envase de cartón carton
48 el jugo juice
49 la galleta cookie
50 la caja box
51 la barra de chocolate, la tableta
    de chocolate chocolate bar
52 la panadería bakery
53 el panadero baker
54 la barra de pan loaf of bread

–¿Me da un kilo de tomates, por favor?
–Could I have a kilo of tomatoes, please?

–¿Va a pagar en efectivo o con tarjeta?
–Cash or credit?

453,59237 gramos (g) = 1 libra
453.59237 grams (g) = 1 pound

28,3495 gramos (g) = 1 onza
28.3495 grams (g) = 1 ounce

Las frutas y las verduras Fruits and Vegetables _____

1 la lechuga lettuce	13 el perejil parsley
2 el tomate tomato	14 el puerro leek
3 la calabaza pumpkin	15 la arveja pea
4 la papa potato	16 la habichuela green bean
5 el ajo garlic	17 el maíz corn
6 la cebolla onion	18 la remolacha beet
7 la zanahoria carrot	19 el rábano radish
8 la espinaca spinach	20 la berenjena eggplant
9 la coliflor cauliflower	21 el espárrago asparagus
10 el brócoli broccoli	22 la alcachofa artichoke
11 el repollo, la col cabbage	23 la acelga Swiss chard
12 el pepino cucumber	24 el apio celery
	25 el pimiento bell pepper

26 estar verde to be unripe,
　 to be green
27 estar maduro to be ripe
28 estar podrido to be rotten
29 el plátano banana
30 la manzana apple
31 la naranja orange
32 el limón, la lima lemon
33 la mandarina mandarin orange,
　 tangerine
34 la lima, el limón lime

35 la piña pineapple
36 la uva grape
37 el higo fig
38 la cereza cherry
39 la sandía watermelon
40 el aguacate avocado
41 el melón melon
42 el durazno peach
43 la pera pear

44 el kiwi kiwi
45 la fresa strawberry
46 la mora blackberry
47 la frambuesa raspberry
48 el arándano blueberry
49 la avellana hazelnut
50 el dátil date
51 el pistacho pistachio
52 la nuez walnut
53 la almendra almond
54 el piñón pine nut
55 el cacahuate, el maní peanut

56 la lenteja lentil
57 el garbanzo chickpea
58 el frijol bean

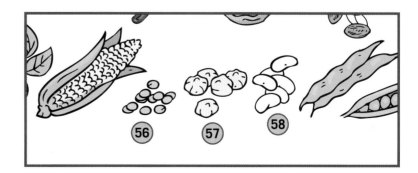

El restaurante The Restaurant

1 **dejar una propina** to leave a tip
2 **desayunar** to have breakfast
3 **el mantel** tablecloth
4 **merendar** to have an afternoon snack
5 **comer** to eat
6 **pedir** to order
7 **almorzar** to have lunch
8 **estar rico, estar delicioso** to be good,
   to be delicious
9 **estar frío** to be cold

10 **traer la cuenta** to bring the check
11 **cocinar** to cook
12 **el cocinero** chef, cook
13 **el mesero, el camarero** waiter
14 **la bandeja** tray
15 **beber** to drink
16 **estar caliente** to be hot
17 **la servilleta** napkin
18 **cenar** to have dinner, to have supper
19 **traer la carta, traer el menú** to bring the menu

20 la taza cup
21 la azucarera, el azucarero sugar bowl
22 la cafetera coffee pot
23 la mermelada jam
24 la mantequilla butter
25 el té tea
26 la jarra pitcher
27 la tetera teapot
28 los cereales cereal
29 el bol bowl
30 el vaso glass

31 el agua water
32 el bistec con papas steak with potatoes
33 el plato fuerte, el segundo plato second course
34 el vinagre vinegar
35 la ensalada salad
36 la entrada, el primer plato first course
37 el pan bread
38 la sal salt
39 la pimienta pepper
40 el aceite oil
41 el postre dessert
42 la tarta de manzana apple pie
43 el helado ice cream
44 el café coffee

45 la sopa soup
46 la sopera soup tureen
47 el plato llano (dinner) plate
48 el plato hondo soup dish
49 la copa wine glass
50 el tenedor fork
51 el cuchillo knife
52 la cuchara spoon

53 la cucharita teaspoon
54 el café con leche coffee with milk
55 el sándwich sandwich
56 la pajita straw

–¿Me puede traer un café, por favor?
–Could I have a coffee, please?

–Quisiera un bistec poco hecho, por favor.
–I'd like a steak cooked rare, please.

–¿Me trae la cuenta, por favor?
–Could I have the check, please?

–Nada más, gracias.
–Nothing else, thank you.

La oficina The Office

1 la empresa company
2 el tablero de anuncios notice board
3 trabajar to work
4 el compañero coworker
5 el secretario secretary
6 dejar un recado to leave a message
7 el despacho office
8 el director, el gerente manager
9 la impresora printer
10 imprimir to print
11 el fax fax

12 enviar un fax to send a fax
13 llegar tarde to arrive late
14 apagar to turn off
15 el empleado employee
16 el jefe boss
17 la reunión meeting
18 reunirse to meet
19 la recepción reception desk
20 firmar to sign
21 llamar por teléfono to talk on the phone

22 tener una cita to have an appointment
23 la tarjeta de presentación business card
24 la fotocopiadora photocopier
25 fotocopiar, hacer fotocopias to photocopy, to make photocopies
26 la trituradora de papel shredder
27 archivar to file

28 el teléfono telephone
29 prender, encender to turn on
30 la *laptop*, la computadora portátil laptop computer
31 el portafolios, el maletín briefcase
32 el (teléfono) celular cell phone

33 la computadora desktop computer
34 la pantalla screen
35 el teclado keyboard
36 el ratón mouse
37 la CPU CPU
38 navegar (por Internet, la red) to surf (the Internet, the Web)

39 escribir un correo electrónico to email
40 la arroba "at" symbol

41 la engrapadora, la grapadora stapler
42 la goma de borrar eraser
43 la cinta adhesiva Scotch tape®, tape
44 la carpeta folder
45 el lápiz pencil
46 el sujetapapeles, el clip paper clip
47 el pegamento glue
48 la hoja sheet
49 el cuaderno notebook
50 la agenda calendar
51 el bolígrafo pen
52 la calculadora calculator

53 la entrevista interview
54 el currículum (CV) résumé, curriculum vitae
55 contratar a alguien to hire someone

—*¿Sí? ¿Dígame?*
—*Hello?*
—*¿Podría hablar con el señor Martínez, por favor?*
—*Could I speak to Mr. Martinez, please?*
—*¿De parte de quién?*
—*Who may I say is calling?*
—*Del señor Sánchez.*
—*Mr. Sanchez.*

—*Un momento, por favor. Ahora le paso.*
—*One moment please. I'll put you through.*
—*Soy Francisco González, de Consultores SR.*
—*I'm Francisco Gonzalez from SR Consultants.*
—*Encantado de conocerlo.*
—*Pleased to meet you.*
—*Mucho gusto.*
—*Nice to meet you.*

1 **pintar** to paint
2 **tejer** to knit
3 **leer una novela** to read a novel
4 **pasear** to go for a walk
5 **patinar** to roller-skate
6 **aplaudir** to applaud, to clap
7 **tomar fotografías** to take photos
8 **el triciclo** tricycle
9 **el muñeco** doll
10 **divertirse** to have fun
11 **aburrirse** to get bored
12 **la patineta** skateboard

13 **jugar a las cartas** to play cards
14 **jugar al ajedrez** to play chess
15 **el bailarín** dancer
16 **la cámara fotográfica, la cámara de fotos** camera
17 **invitar** to treat someone, to pay for someone
18 **quedar** to arrange to meet, to meet (up with)
19 **bailar** to dance
20 **jugar a las escondidas** to play hide-and-go-seek
21 **la cafetería** café
22 **tomar algo** to have a drink

23 el cuadro painting
24 la exposición exhibition
25 visitar una exposición to see an exhibition
26 el museo museum
27 la escultura sculpture

28 el teatro theater
29 el escenario stage
30 la escenografía, el decorado scenery
31 la obra de teatro play

32 el cine movie theater
33 la boletería, la taquilla box office
34 el boleto ticket
35 ir al cine to go to the movies
36 la butaca seat
37 la película film

38 el concierto concert
39 el músico musician
40 el piano piano
41 tocar un instrumento to play an instrument
42 la trompeta trumpet
43 el violín violin
44 la orquesta orchestra
45 cantar to sing
46 el cantante singer
47 la guitarra guitar
48 el director conductor
49 escuchar música to listen to music

50 el columpio swing
51 el tobogán slide
52 el carrusel merry-go-round, carousel
53 saltar a la cuerda to skip
54 el papalote, la cometa kite
55 el subibaja seesaw

–¿Qué le gusta hacer en su tiempo libre?
–What do you like to do in your free time?
–Me gusta mucho leer y pasear.
–I like reading and going for walks a lot.

–¿Toca algún instrumento?
–Do you play any musical instruments?
–Sí, toco el piano.
–Yes, I play the piano.

1 el fútbol americano football	12 la camiseta T-shirt
2 el béisbol baseball	13 el pantalón corto shorts
3 correr to run	14 las zapatillas de tenis sneakers, tennis shoes
4 el atletismo track and field	15 el tenis tennis
5 el golf golf	16 la natación swimming
6 el palo de golf golf club	17 descansar to rest
7 empatar to tie	18 montar en bicicleta to ride a bike
8 el basquetbol, el básquetbol basketball	19 el ciclismo cycling
9 perder to lose	20 el casco helmet
10 ganar to win	21 la bicicleta bicycle
11 el fútbol soccer	22 la sudadera sweatsuit

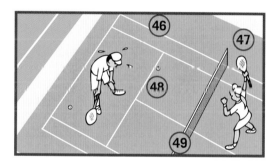

23 la cancha, el campo de fútbol court, field
24 el entrenador coach
25 el portero, el arquero goalkeeper
26 la portería, el arco goal
27 meter un gol to score a goal
28 jugar al fútbol to play soccer
29 el jugador player
30 el árbitro referee

31 el trampolín diving board
32 el gorro swim cap
33 las gafas goggles
34 un clavado, tirarse de cabeza to dive
35 nadar estilo mariposa to swim butterfly
36 nadar estilo espalda to swim (the) backstroke
37 la piscina swimming pool
38 nadar estilo pecho to swim (the) breaststroke

39 nadar to swim
40 nadar estilo crol to swim the crawl

41 pasar (la pelota) to pass (the ball)
42 saltar to jump
43 la canasta basket
44 el marcador scoreboard
45 el equipo team

46 la cancha de tenis tennis court
47 la raqueta racket
48 la pelota ball
49 la red net

50 las pesas weights
51 hacer ejercicio to exercise
52 el gimnasio gym, gymnasium

53 el bate bat
54 el guante de béisbol baseball glove
55 la gorra cap
56 lanzar (la pelota) to throw (the ball)

–¿Qué deportes practica?
–What sports do you play?

–Nado dos veces a la semana y juego tenis los sábados.
–I swim twice a week and I play tennis on Saturdays.

1 la primavera spring	11 el verano summer
2 el cielo sky	12 el sol sun
3 la nube cloud	13 hacer viento to be windy
4 el campo countryside	14 hacer calor to be hot
5 el otoño fall	15 la playa beach
6 llover to rain	16 el invierno winter
7 haber tormenta there's a storm, to be stormy	17 la luna moon
	18 la estrella star
8 el bosque forest	19 nevar to snow
9 haber niebla to be foggy	20 la montaña mountain
10 estar nublado to be cloudy, to be overcast	21 hacer frío to be cold

22	el barco de vela sailboat	
23	el chaleco salvavidas life vest	
24	el salvavidas lifeguard	
25	ponerse bloqueador solar to put on sunscreen	
26	el flotador float ring	
27	el mar sea	
28	hacer buceo, bucear to go scuba diving	
29	hacer surf to surf	
30	la ola wave	
31	la orilla shore	
32	la sombrilla beach umbrella	

33 la arena sand
34 tomar el sol to sunbathe

35 el lago lake
36 ir en canoa to go canoeing
37 montar a caballo to ride horses, to go horseback riding
38 el pasto grass
39 el saco de dormir sleeping bag
40 la carpa tent
41 la linterna flashlight
42 la cantimplora canteen
43 acampar to camp, to go camping
44 escalar to climb

45 la cascada waterfall
46 el río river
47 pescar to fish, to go fishing
48 la caña de pescar fishing rod
49 hacer senderismo to hike, to go hiking
50 el árbol tree

51 el valle valley
52 el pueblo town, village
53 el establo stable
54 el tractor tractor
55 el muñeco de nieve snowman
56 esquiar to ski, to go skiing

–¿Qué van a hacer este fin de semana?
–What are you going to do this weekend?

–El sábado vamos a ir al mar a bucear.
–On Saturday we are going to the beach to go scuba diving.

–¡Qué calor hace!
–It's so hot!

–Mañana estará nublado y hará frío en todo el país. La temperatura máxima será de diez grados (10 °C).
–Tomorrow is going to be cold and cloudy all across the country. Temperatures will reach a maximum of 10 °C.

0 °C (grados Celcius) = 32 °F (grados Fahrenheit)
0 °C (degrees Celcius) = 32 °F (degrees Fahrenheit)

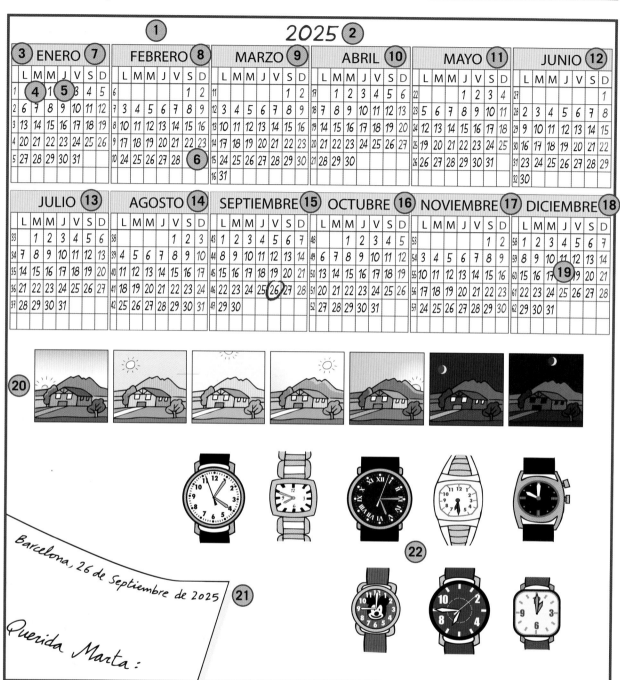

2025

1 el calendario calendar	12 junio June
2 el año year	13 julio July
3 el mes month	14 agosto August
4 el día feriado holiday	15 septiembre September
5 el Año Nuevo New Year's Day	16 octubre October
6 la semana week	17 noviembre November
7 enero January	18 diciembre December
8 febrero February	19 la Navidad Christmas
9 marzo March	20 el día day
10 abril April	21 la fecha date
11 mayo May	22 la hora hour

23 el lunes Monday
24 el martes Tuesday
25 el miércoles Wednesday
26 el jueves Thursday
27 el viernes Friday
28 el sábado Saturday
29 el domingo Sunday
30 el fin de semana weekend

31 hoy today
32 ayer yesterday
33 mañana tomorrow
34 antes de ayer the day before yesterday
35 pasado mañana the day after tomorrow

36 amanecer to get light
37 en la mañana, por la mañana in the morning
38 al mediodía at noon
39 en la tarde, por la tarde in the afternoon, in the evening
40 atardecer to get dark
41 en la noche, por la noche at night
42 a medianoche at midnight

43 el segundo second
44 el minuto minute
45 es la una en punto it's exactly one o'clock
46 son las cuatro y cinco it's five after four
47 son las cinco y cuarto it's quarter after five
48 son las seis y media it's six thirty
49 falta un cuarto para las siete, son las siete menos cuarto it's quarter of seven, it's quarter till seven
50 faltan diez para las ocho, son las ocho menos diez it's ten of eight
51 son las nueve de la mañana it's nine o'clock in the morning, it's nine a.m.
52 son las diez de la noche it's ten o'clock at night, it's ten p.m.

–¿Qué hora es?
–What time is it?
–Son las dos y media.
–It's two thirty.

–¿A qué hora abren las tiendas?
–What time do the stores open?
–A las nueve de la mañana.
–At nine a.m.

–¿Qué día es hoy?
–What's the day today?
–Hoy es diez de enero.
–Today is the tenth of January.

–El metro cierra de las dos a las seis de la mañana.
–The subway is closed from two to six in the morning.

–¿Cuándo va al gimnasio?
–When do you go to the gym?
–Voy los martes y los jueves por la tarde.
–I go on Tuesday and Thursday afternoons.

–¡Feliz Navidad!   –¡Feliz Año Nuevo!
–Merry Christmas!   –Happy New Year!

Describir cosas Describing Things

1 ser cuadrado to be square
2 ser redondo to be round
3 estar grande, ser grande to be large, to be big
4 estar pequeño, ser pequeño to be small,
   to be little
5 estar viejo, ser viejo to be old
6 estar nuevo, ser nuevo to be new
7 uno one
8 dos two
9 tres three
10 cuatro four

11 cinco five
12 seis six
13 siete seven
14 ocho eight
15 nueve nine
16 diez ten
17 once eleven
18 doce twelve
19 trece thirteen
20 catorce fourteen
21 quince fifteen

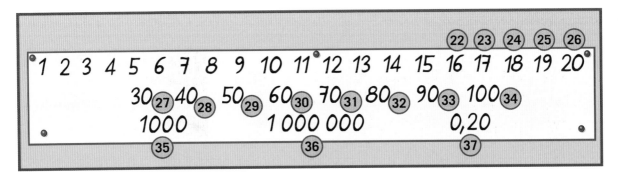

22	dieciséis sixteen	26	veinte twenty	30	sesenta sixty	34	cien a hundred
23	diecisiete seventeen	27	treinta thirty	31	setenta seventy	35	mil a thousand
24	dieciocho eighteen	28	cuarenta forty	32	ochenta eighty	36	un millón a million
25	diecinueve nineteen	29	cincuenta fifty	33	noventa ninety	37	cero con veinte zero point twenty

38 primero first
39 segundo second
40 tercero third
41 cuarto fourth
42 quinto fifth
43 sexto sixth
44 séptimo seventh
45 octavo eighth
46 noveno ninth
47 décimo tenth

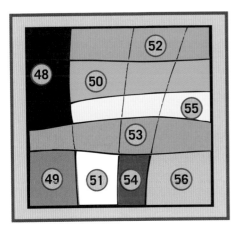

48 ser negro to be black
49 ser café to be brown
50 ser verde to be green
51 ser blanco to be white
52 ser azul to be blue
53 ser anaranjado to be orange
54 ser rojo to be red
55 ser amarillo to be yellow
56 ser gris to be gray

–Veinte menos quince son cinco.
–Twenty minus fifteen is five.

–Trece más siete son veinte.
–Thirteen plus seven is twenty.

–Tres por cuatro son doce.
–Three times four is twelve.

–Veinticuatro entre seis son cuatro.
–Twenty-four divided by six is four.

El auto y la carretera The Car and the Road

1 el túnel tunnel	12 la autopista freeway
2 la señal de tráfico traffic sign	13 la camioneta, la furgoneta van
3 frenar to brake, to stop	14 el camión truck
4 el carril lane	15 acelerar to accelerate
5 el acotamiento, el arcén shoulder	16 la salida exit
6 el convertible, el descapotable convertible	17 el peaje toll
7 conducir to drive	18 la carretera highway
8 pasar, adelantar to pass	19 el área de servicio service
9 ir rápido to go fast, to speed	station
10 el puente overpass	20 arrancar to start (up)
11 la curva curve	21 estacionarse to park

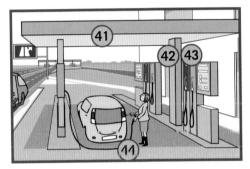

22 el capó hood
23 la batería battery
24 el motor engine
25 el radiador radiator
26 la placa, la matrícula licence plate
27 la luz headlight
28 las defensas, el parachoques bumper
29 la llanta, la rueda tire, wheel
30 el rin, la llanta hubcap
31 los limpiaparabrisas windshield wipers
32 el parabrisas windshield
33 el asiento seat
34 el cinturón de seguridad seat belt
35 la cajuela, el maletero trunk
36 el direccional, el intermitente turn signal
37 el claxon, la bocina horn
38 el volante steering wheel
39 la guantera glove compartment

40 la caja de velocidades, la caja de cambios stick shift
41 la gasolinera gas station
42 el diésel, el gasoil diesel (fuel)
43 la gasolina gas
44 llenar el tanque to fill the tank
45 el gato jack
46 pinchar una llanta to get a flat tire
47 inflar la llanta to put air in the tire
48 el embotellamiento, el atasco traffic jam
49 la licencia de conducir driver's license
50 la infracción, la multa ticket
51 chocar to crash
52 el choque crash, accident
53 empujar to push
54 descomponerse, averiarse to break down
55 la grúa tow truck

–Mi auto se descompuso. ¿Podría enviar una grúa, por favor?
–My car has broken down. Could you send a tow truck, please?
–Lleno, por favor. Gasolina sin plomo.
–Fill her up, please. Unleaded.

1,6 kilómetros (km) = 1 milla
1.6 kilometers (km) = 1 mile
0,91 metros (m) = 1 yarda (yd)
0.91 meters (m) = 1 yard (yd)

De viaje Traveling

1 **recoger el equipaje** to pick up the luggage
2 **llegadas** arrivals
3 **el piloto** pilot
4 **el auxiliar de vuelo, la azafata** flight attendant
5 **el pasajero** passenger
6 **el mapa** map
7 **el país** country
8 **la capital** capital (city)
9 **el pasaporte** passport
10 **el boleto de avión** ticket
11 **perder el avión** to miss the plane

12 **el aeropuerto** airport
13 **despedirse** to say good-bye
14 **la aduana** Customs
15 **revisar el equipaje** to check luggage
16 **esperar** to wait
17 **salidas** departures
18 **la puerta de embarque** gate
19 **embarcar** to board
20 **la pista de aterrizaje** runway
21 **aterrizar** to land
22 **despegar** to take off
23 **volar** to fly

24 la oficina de cambio exchange bureau
25 cambiar dinero to exchange money
26 el destino destination
27 el vuelo flight
28 la compañía aérea airline
29 facturar el equipaje to check in luggage
30 el mostrador counter
31 el equipaje baggage, luggage
32 la maleta suitcase
33 el carrito cart
34 la tarjeta de embarque boarding pass
35 la mochila backpack

36 el guía turístico tour guide
37 la oficina de turismo tourist bureau
38 mirar un mapa, consultar un mapa
to look at a map, to check a map

39 el turista tourist

40 el avión airplane
41 la cola tail
42 el ala wing
43 la ventanilla window

44 el servicio de habitaciones
room service
45 la habitación individual single room
46 hacer las maletas to pack (suitcases, bags)
47 la habitación doble double room
48 deshacer las maletas to unpack (suitcase, bags)
49 el hotel hotel
50 hacer una reservación, hacer una reserva
to make a reservation
51 el recepcionista receptionist
52 la recepción reception

–Quisiera reservar una habitación doble del veintisiete
al treinta de marzo, por favor.
–I'd like to reserve a double room for the twenty-seventh
to the thirtieth of March, please.

–Quisiera una habitación con vistas a la playa, por favor.
–I'd like a room with a view of the beach, please.

–¡Buen viaje!
–Have a nice trip!

–No tengo nada que declarar.
–I have nothing to declare.

–Usted tiene exceso de equipaje.
–You have excess baggage.

–Por favor, abróchense los cinturones de seguridad.
–Please fasten your seatbelts.

1 recibir una carta to receive a letter
2 el telegrama telegram
3 entregar un telegrama to deliver a telegram
4 abrir una carta to open a letter
5 robar to steal (something), to rob (a person or place)
6 el mensajero messenger, courier
7 la tarjeta de crédito credit card
8 el paquete package
9 repartir el correo to deliver the mail, to post
10 el cartero mailman
11 la oficina de correos post office
12 enviar un paquete to send a package

13 la postal postcard
14 el correo certificado certified mail
15 cerrar una carta to seal a letter
16 el correo urgente priority mail
17 la billetera wallet
18 el billete bill
19 el cajero automático automated teller machine (ATM)
20 la tarjeta de débito debit card
21 el banco bank
22 el dinero money
23 la moneda coin

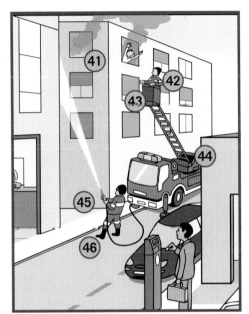

24 sacar dinero to withdraw money, to take out money
25 la alarma alarm
26 la cartilla passbook
27 el guardia de seguridad security guard
28 el estado de cuenta, el extracto statement
29 el cheque check
30 la ventanilla window
31 depositar dinero to deposit money

32 el sobre envelope
33 la carta letter
34 el remitente sender
35 la dirección address
36 el nombre first name
37 el apellido last name
38 el timbre, el sello stamp
39 el destinatario addressee
40 el código postal ZIP code

41 el incendio fire
42 el bombero fireman
43 ayudar to help
44 el camión de bomberos fire truck
45 la manguera hose
46 apagar un incendio to put out a fire

47 la comisaría police station
48 detener to arrest
49 el policía police officer
50 la patrulla patrol car

–Quisiera abrir una cuenta, por favor.
–I'd like to open an account, please.

–Me han robado la tarjeta de crédito y quería cancelarla.
–My credit card has been stolen and I'd like to cancel it.

–Quisiera enviar esta carta urgente y certificada, por favor.
–I'd like to send this letter by certified and priority mail.

–¡Socorro!
–Help!

Los animales Animals

1 el gato cat	10 la oveja sheep	19 croar to croak
2 maullar to mew	11 balar to bleat	20 picar to sting,
3 el perro dog	12 ser herbívoro to be herbivorous,	to bite
4 ladrar to bark	to be grass-eating	21 el león lion
5 la vaca cow	13 el cerdo pig	22 ser salvaje to be wild
6 mugir to moo	14 la gallina hen	23 ser carnívoro to be carnivorous,
7 ser manso to be tame,	15 cacarear to crow, to cluck	meat-eating
domesticated	16 el pájaro bird	24 rugir to roar
8 el caballo horse	17 piar to chirp, to tweet	25 ser venenoso
9 relinchar to neigh, to whinny	18 la rana frog	to be poisonous

26 el águila eagle
27 el oso bear
28 la mariposa butterfly
29 la abeja bee
30 el caracol snail
31 el mosquito mosquito
32 el conejo rabbit
33 el lobo wolf

34 el elefante elephant
35 el hipopótamo hippopotamus
36 la jirafa giraffe
37 la cebra zebra
38 el cocodrilo crocodile

39 el loro parrot
40 el mono monkey
41 la serpiente snake
42 el tigre tiger

43 el pingüino penguin
44 la foca seal
45 el delfín dolphin
46 la ballena whale
47 la tortuga turtle
48 el pez fish
49 el pulpo octopus
50 la estrella de mar starfish
51 el tiburón shark

52 el hocico snout, muzzle
53 el lomo back
54 la pata leg
55 la cola tail

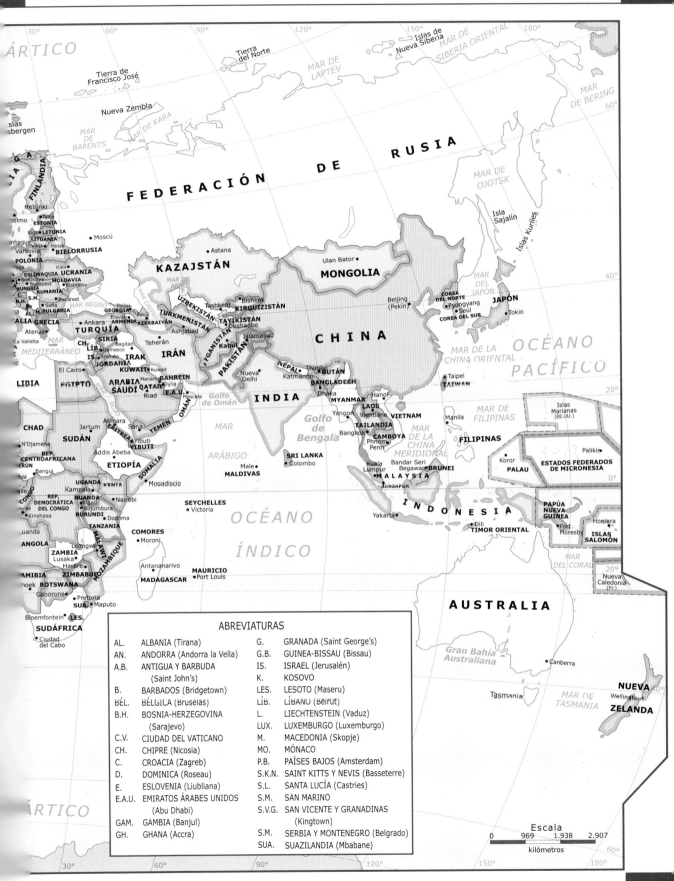

ABREVIATURAS

AL.   ALBANIA (Tirana)
AN.   ANDORRA (Andorra la Vella)
A.B.   ANTIGUA Y BARBUDA
       (Saint John's)
B.   BARBADOS (Bridgetown)
BÉL.   BÉLGICA (Bruselas)
B.H.   BOSNIA-HERZEGOVINA
       (Sarajevo)
C.V.   CIUDAD DEL VATICANO
CH.   CHIPRE (Nicosia)
C.   CROACIA (Zagreb)
D.   DOMINICA (Roseau)
E.   ESLOVENIA (Liubliana)
E.A.U. EMIRATOS ÁRABES UNIDOS
       (Abu Dhabi)
GAM.   GAMBIA (Banjul)
GH.   GHANA (Accra)

G.   GRANADA (Saint George's)
G.B.   GUINEA-BISSAU (Bissau)
IS.   ISRAEL (Jerusalén)
K.   KOSOVO
LES.   LESOTO (Maseru)
LÍB.   LÍBANO (Beirut)
L.   LIECHTENSTEIN (Vaduz)
LUX.   LUXEMBURGO (Luxemburgo)
M.   MACEDONIA (Skopje)
MO.   MÓNACO
P.B.   PAÍSES BAJOS (Amsterdam)
S.K.N. SAINT KITTS Y NEVIS (Basseterre)
S.L.   SANTA LUCÍA (Castries)
S.M.   SAN MARINO
S.V.G. SAN VICENTE Y GRANADINAS
       (Kingtown)
S.M.   SERBIA Y MONTENEGRO (Belgrado)
SUA.   SUAZILANDIA (Mbabane)

Escala
0   969   1.938   2.907
kilómetros

El mundo The World

1 Norte North
2 Sur South
3 Oriente, Este East
4 Occidente, Oeste West

5 Antártida Antarctica
6 América del Norte North America
7 América del Sur South America
8 África Africa
9 Europa Europe
10 Asia Asia
11 Oceanía Oceania

12 Océano Atlántico Atlantic Ocean
13 Océano Pacífico Pacific Ocean
14 Océano Índico Indian Ocean

15 Canadá: canadiense Canada: Canadian
16 Los Estados Unidos: estadounidense The United
   States of America: American
17 México: mexicano Mexico: Mexican

18 Marruecos: marroquí Morocco: Moroccan
19 Egipto: egipcio Egypt: Egyptian
20 Suráfrica: surafricano South Africa: South African

21 China: chino China: Chinese
22 India: indio India: Indian
23 Japón: japonés Japan: Japanese

24 Australia: australiano Australia: Australian

25 Guatemala: guatemalteco Guatemala: Guatemalan
26 El Salvador: salvadoreño El Salvador: Salvadorian
27 Honduras: hondureño Honduras: Honduran
28 Nicaragua: nicaragüense Nicaragua: Nicaraguan
29 Costa Rica: costarricense Costa Rica: Costa Rican
30 Panamá: panameño Panama: Panamanian

31 Cuba: cubano Cuba: Cuban
32 Haití: haitiano Haiti: Haitian
33 República Dominicana: dominicano
   Dominican Republic: Dominican
34 Venezuela: venezolano Venezuela: Venezuelan
35 Colombia: colombiano Colombia: Colombian
36 Ecuador: ecuatoriano Ecuador: Ecuadorian
37 Perú: peruano Peru: Peruvian
38 Bolivia: boliviano Bolivia: Bolivian
39 Chile: chileno Chile: Chilean
40 Argentina: argentino Argentina: Argentinian
41 Uruguay: uruguayo Uruguay: Uruguayan
42 Paraguay: paraguayo Paraguay: Paraguayan
43 Brasil: brasileño Brazil: Brazilian

44 España: español Spain: Spanish
45 Francia: francés France: French
46 Alemania: alemán Germany: German
47 Bélgica: belga Belgium: Belgian
48 Países Bajos (Holanda): holandés
   The Netherlands (Holland): Dutch
49 Reino Unido: británico United Kingdom:
   British
50 Irlanda: irlandés Ireland: Irish
51 Dinamarca: danés Denmark: Danish
52 Noruega: noruego Norway: Norwegian
53 Suecia: sueco Sweden: Swedish
54 Suiza: suizo Switzerland: Swiss
55 Austria: austriaco Austria: Austrian
56 Polonia: polaco Poland: Polish
57 Italia: italiano Italy: Italian
58 Grecia: griego Greece: Greek
59 Turquía: turco Turkey: Turkish
60 Rusia: ruso Russia: Russian

Las lenguas

el alemán German
el árabe Arabic
el bengalí Bengali
el chino Chinese
el coreano Korean
el español Spanish
el francés French
el hindi Hindi
el inglés English

el italiano Italian
el japonés Japanese
el javanés Javanese
el polaco Polish
el portugués Portuguese
el ruso Russian
el turco Turkish
el urdu Urdu
el vietnamita Vietnamese

–¿De dónde es usted?
–Where are you from?
–Soy mexicano, de Puebla.
–I'm Mexican, from Puebla.

–¿Sabe cuál es la capital de Chile?
–Do you know what the capital of Chile is?
–Sí, Santiago.
–Yes, Santiago.

–¿Conoce Guatemala?
–Have you ever been to Guatemala?
–Sí, estuve allí el verano pasado.
–Yes, I was there last summer.

–¿Habla usted español?
–Do you speak Spanish?
–Sí, hablo español y francés.
–Yes, I speak Spanish and French.

1 Look at this family tree and complete the sentences.

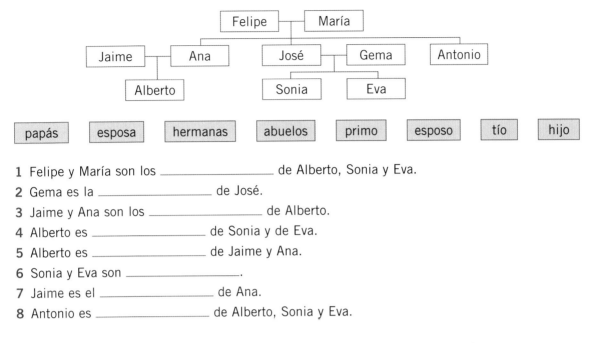

| papás | esposa | hermanas | abuelos | primo | esposo | tío | hijo |

1 Felipe y María son los _____ de Alberto, Sonia y Eva.

2 Gema es la _____ de José.

3 Jaime y Ana son los _____ de Alberto.

4 Alberto es _____ de Sonia y de Eva.

5 Alberto es _____ de Jaime y Ana.

6 Sonia y Eva son _____.

7 Jaime es el _____ de Ana.

8 Antonio es _____ de Alberto, Sonia y Eva.

2 Look at the pictures, unscramble the letters and complete the verbs.

1 asoatcrse

_____

2 ebarsañ

_____

3 nelaevatrs

_____

4 setsvire

_____

5 neipsear

_____

6 velrasa

_____ los dientes

3 In what order do you do these everyday actions? Write them down.

1 _____

2 _____

3 _____

4 _____

5 _____

6 acostarse

Soluciones: 1. 1 abuelos; 2 esposa/mujer; 3 papás; 4 primo; 5 hijo; 6 hermanas; 7 esposo/marido; 8 tío. **2.** 1 acostarse; 2 bañarse; 3 levantarse; 4 vestirse; 5 peinarse; 6 lavarse los dientes.

1 Mark the words that are illustrated in the pictures.

☐ ser mayor
☐ ser joven

☐ ser bajo
☐ ser alto

☐ ser gordo
☐ ser delgado

☐ tener canas
☐ estar calvo

☐ tener pelo rubio
☐ tener pelo negro

☐ tener barba
☐ tener bigote

☐ tener pelo corto
☐ tener pelo largo

☐ estar bronceado
☐ tener pecas

☐ tener pelo liso
☐ tener pelo rizado

☐ tener colitas
☐ tener trenzas

☐ tener ojos claros
☐ tener ojos oscuros

☐ adulto
☐ viejito

Soluciones: 1. 1 ser mayor; 2 ser alto; 3 ser delgado; 4 estar calvo; 5 tener pelo rubio; 6 tener bigote; 7 tener pelo corto; 8 tener pecas; 9 tener pelo rizado; 10 tener colitas; 11 tener ojos claros; 12 viejito.

1 Look at the pictures, match them with their opposites and write what they are.

1 estar tranquilo

a _____

2 ser sociable

b _____

3 ser generoso

c _____

4 reír

d _____

5 tener calor

e _____

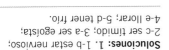

Soluciones: 1. 1-b estar nervioso;
2-c ser tímido; 3-a ser egoísta;
4-e llorar, 5-d tener frío.

1 Look at the pictures and complete the crossword puzzle.

2 Unscramble the letters to spell these pieces of clothing and accessories.

1 la **taabocr** _____
2 el **tdioves** _____
3 la **mciasa** _____
4 el **leorj** _____

5 la **tijasor** _____
6 la **absol** _____
7 la **apmija** _____
8 la **usplrae** _____

3 Complete the words. Then match them with their opposites.

1 estar l__r__o
2 estar __n__ __o
3 ser b__n__t__

a estar __s__r__ch__
b ser __e__
c estar c__r__o

1 Look at the pictures and complete the sentences.

1 La veterinaria trabaja en una _____.

2 El _____ trabaja en un estudio.

3 El abogado trabaja en un _____.

4 El _____ trabaja en un taller.

5 El empresario tiene una _____.

6 El _____ trabaja en casa.

7 El científico trabaja en un _____.

8 El _____ conduce un camión.

9 La psicóloga trabaja en un _____.

10 La _____ da clase en una universidad.

Soluciones: 1. 1 clínica; 2 arquitecto; 3 bufete; 4 mecánico; 5 fábrica/empresa; 6 ama de casa; 7 laboratorio; 8 camionero; 9 consultorio; 10 profesora.

1 Look at the pictures and try to find these words in the word search.

D	R	T	G	H	Y	U	J	K	I	H	F	T
P	M	E	D	I	C	A	M	E	N	T	O	E
U	J	K	I	H	F	C	L	A	D	E	E	R
E	Y	A	M	B	U	L	A	N	C	I	A	M
C	P	K	O	S	T	D	C	S	M	E	D	Ó
S	A	L	A	D	E	E	S	P	E	R	A	M
F	C	Ñ	M	E	L	N	D	V	W	E	B	E
V	I	G	H	N	D	F	H	F	S	C	G	T
H	E	T	T	E	E	O	R	D	E	T	R
R	N	R	F	I	N	R	S	E	R	T	Y	O
S	T	D	C	S	F	M	P	D	T	A	H	A
A	E	S	O	T	E	E	I	C	T	O	N	K
A	J	Z	B	A	E	R	R	S	H	I	M	I
R	T	G	H	Y	U	A	F	X	N	M	J	Z

2 Complete the names of the parts of the body. Afterwards, place them in the table.

1 c__b__z__
2 __a__o
3 p__ __rn__
4 __r__z__
5 d__ __o

6 ga__g__ __t__
7 __st__m__ __ __ __
8 r__d__l__a
9 __u__la
10 __i__

El	
La	

1 Look at the pictures and complete the crossword puzzle.

2 Match the opposites.

1 cerca   a cerrado
2 delante   b lejos
3 arriba   c atrás
4 abierto   d abajo

---

1 Look at the pictures. Then write the name of each piece of furniture or household appliance in the right place. Afterwards, write the corresponding article *(el, la)* next to each word.

sofá	cama	mesa	refrigerador	ducha

sillón	armario	lavabo	lavaplatos	silla

1 _____

_____

2 _____

_____

3 _____

_____

4 _____

_____

5 _____

_____

2 Complete the name of the rooms shown in the previous exercise with the missing letters.

1 el c__m__d__r   2 la s__l__

3 la c__c__n__   4 la h__b__t__c__ón   5 el c____rt__ de b__ñ__

3 Match the columns to form verb phrases.

1 limpiar   a la cama

2 lavar   b limpio

3 lavar en   c la casa

4 tender   d los platos

5 estar   e la lavadora

1 Look at the pictures and complete the crossword puzzle.

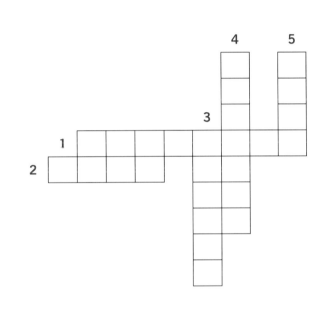

2 Complete these words with the missing letters.

1 el p__rqu__
2 la p__r__d__ de __ __t__bús
3 la c__ll__

4 el __st__c__ __n__m__ __nt__
5 el cr__c__ p__ __t__n__l
6 la __st__c__ __n d__ m__tr__

3 Write the opposite of each verb.

1 entrar ↔ _____
2 preguntar ↔ _____

3 subir ↔ _____
4 dar vuelta a la derecha ↔ _____

1 Look at the pictures and write the name below each picture.

escaparate	ticket	peluquero	etiqueta	papelería

bolsa	agencia de viajes	ramo de rosas

1 el _____

2 el _____

3 la _____

4 la _____

5 el _____

6 el _____

7 la _____

8 la _____

2 Unscramble the letters of the words below. Then match each word with its definition.

1 la **fumíaerrpe** _____

2 la **lirríaeb** _____

3 el **potesu ed socipódire** _____

4 las **cessaaler sacitrecél** _____

5 la **fiaaracm** _____

6 la **zapla crcealomi** _____

7 la **queperíalu** _____

8 la **yejoría** _____

a Lugar donde puedes encontrar muchas tiendas.

b Lugar donde compras libros.

c Lugar donde puedes comprar el periódico.

d Lugar donde compras medicamentos.

e Las usas para subir o bajar de un piso a otro.

f Lugar donde puedes comprar una sortija.

g Lugar donde te pueden cortar el pelo.

h Lugar donde compras perfumes y cremas.

Soluciones: 1. 1 el escaparate; 2 el ramo de rosas; 3 la agencia de viajes;
4 la etiqueta; 5 el ticket; 6 el peluquero; 7 la bolsa; 8 la papelería.
2. 1 la perfumería-h; 2 la librería-b; 3 el puesto de periódicos-c; 4 las escaleras eléctricas-e;
5 la farmacia-d; 6 la plaza comercial-a; 7 la peluquería-g; 8 la joyería-f.

1 Mark the word that does not belong in each group.

1 el yogur ~ la leche ~ el queso ~ el arroz
2 el jugo ~ el pollo ~ la leche ~ el aceite
3 la botella ~ la lata ~ la caja ~ el marisco
4 el litro ~ los congelados ~ la carnicería ~ la frutería
5 la carne de res ~ el pollo ~ el pescado ~ el cerdo

2 Look at the picture and unscramble the letters.

1 la **aptas** _____
2 las **tasgalle** _____
3 los **oshuve** _____
4 la **rinaha** _____
5 el **zorar** _____
6 el **cotachelo** _____

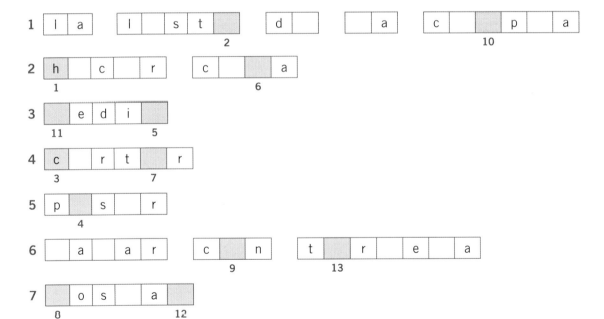

3 Complete the words to discover the mystery phrase.

1 | l | a | | l | | s | t | ☐² | | d | | | | a | | c | | ☐¹⁰ | p | a

2 | h¹ | | c | | r | | | c | | ☐⁶ | a

3 | ☐¹¹ | e | d | i | ☐⁵

4 | c³ | | r | t | ☐⁷ | r

5 | p | | s | | r
       4

6 | | a | | a | r | | c | | n⁹ | | t | | r¹³ | | e | | a

7 | ☐⁸ | o | s | | a | ☐¹²

Hidden Word:

| 1 | 2 | 3 | 4 | 5 | | 6 | 7 | | 8 | 9 | 10 | 11 | 12 | 13 |

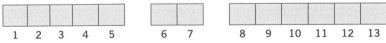

Soluciones: 1. 1 el arroz; 2 el pollo; 3 el marisco; 4 el litro; 5 el pescado.
2. 1 la pasta; 2 las galletas; 3 los huevos; 4 la harina; 5 el arroz; 6 el chocolate.
3. 1 la lista de la compra; 2 hacer cola; 3 pedir; 4 cortar; 5 pesar; 6 pagar con tarjeta;
7 costar. Palabra escondida: hacer la compra.

1 Mark the words that are illustrated in the pictures.

☐ la naranja
☐ la mandarina

☐ la coliflor
☐ el brócoli

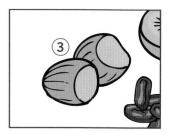

☐ la nuez
☐ la avellana

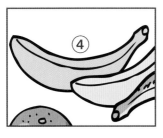

☐ estar verde
☐ estar maduro

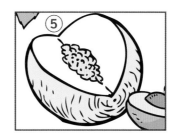

☐ la sandía
☐ el melón

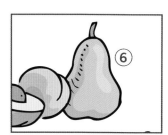

☐ la manzana
☐ la pera

☐ la fresa
☐ la frambuesa

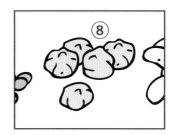

☐ el garbanzo
☐ la lenteja

☐ la cebolla
☐ el ajo

☐ la berenjena
☐ el pimiento

☐ la uva
☐ la cereza

☐ el aguacate
☐ la piña

Soluciones: 1. 1 la naranja; 2 la coliflor; 3 la avellana;
4 estar verde; 5 el melón; 6 la pera; 7 la fresa; 8 el garbanzo;
9 la cebolla; 10 el pimiento; 11 la cereza; 12 la piña.

1 Unscramble the letters of the products. Then organize them in the table according to when you eat them.

1 los **elaserec**

_____

2 la **esanaadl**

_____

3 la **posa**

_____

4 el **éafc**

_____

5 el **nap**

_____

6 la **artat ed zanmana**

_____

7 la **emdramlae**

_____

8 el **cistbe noc paspa**

_____

9 la **lliquanamte**

_____

Desayunar	Almorzar	Merendar	Cenar

2 What do you use to...? Complete the crossword puzzle.

1 Se usa para tomar el postre.

2 Sirve para beber agua.

3 Sirve para tomar la sopa.

4 Sirve para comer la ensalada.

5 Se utiliza para cortar.

6 Se usa para beber el café.

1 Mark the word that does not belong in each group.

1 la impresora ~ el jefe ~ la fotocopiadora ~ el teléfono ~ el fax
2 el cuaderno ~ el bolígrafo ~ el lápiz ~ el despacho ~ la carpeta
3 el director ~ el empleado ~ la entrevista ~ la secretaria ~ el compañero
4 el despacho ~ la empresa ~ la recepción ~ el currículum

2 Look at the pictures. Then unscramble the letters of these verbs.

1 arrtajba

2 irrimmip

3 paraga

4 aiachrvr

5 rfiarm

6 drepren

7 rivean nu xaf

8 eurnsire

9 marall rop tolefoné

10 lelgra aetdr

11 trene anu tica

12 fropiatoco

Soluciones: 1. 1 el jefe; 2 el despacho; 3 la entrevista; 4 el currículum.
2. 1 trabajar; 2 imprimir; 3 apagar; 4 archivar; 5 firmar; 6 prender; 7 enviar un fax;
8 reunirse; 9 llamar por teléfono; 10 llegar tarde; 11 tener una cita; 12 fotocopiar.

1 Unscramble the letters to write the words shown in the pictures.
Then match the related drawings in both columns.

1 tociercon _____

2 tebloo _____

3 calípelu _____

4 ucador _____

5 naserioce _____

a trapin _____

b atrote _____

c llaquati _____

d enci _____

e cimúso _____

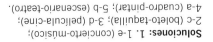

Soluciones: 1. 1-e (concierto-músico);
2-c (boleto-taquilla); 3-d (película-cine);
4-a (cuadro-pintar); 5-b (escenario-teatro).

1 Look at the pictures and match the verbs.

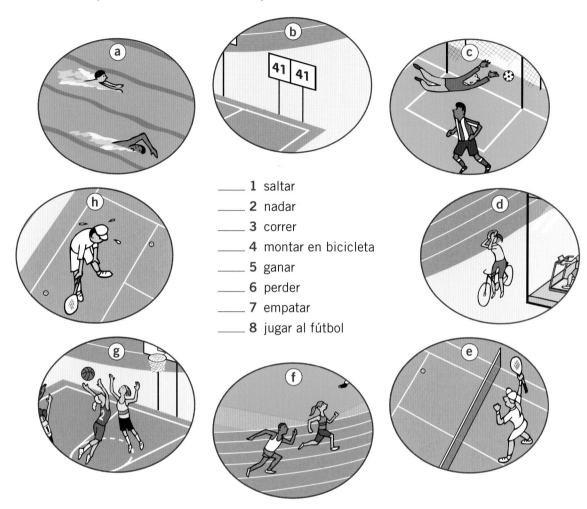

_____ 1 saltar
_____ 2 nadar
_____ 3 correr
_____ 4 montar en bicicleta
_____ 5 ganar
_____ 6 perder
_____ 7 empatar
_____ 8 jugar al fútbol

2 Classify the words by putting them in the table.

| la camiseta | la portería | el béisbol | el casco | la natación | el fútbol |

| el atletismo | la bicicleta | la raqueta | el bate | el ciclismo |

| el tenis | el basquetbol |

Deportes	Material de deporte

---

1 Write each word with its article *(el, la)* under the right picture.
Be careful! There are more words than pictures!

mar	arena	montaña	árbol	bosque

luna	cielo	nube	sol	río

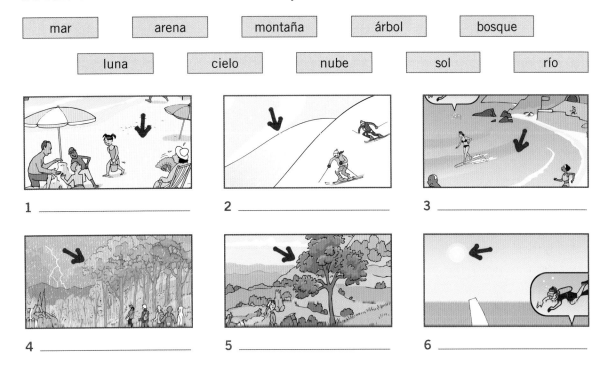

1 _____   2 _____   3 _____

4 _____   5 _____   6 _____

2 What's the weather like? Match the words with the right picture.

① llover   ② nevar   ③ haber tormenta   ④ hacer frío   ⑤ hacer calor

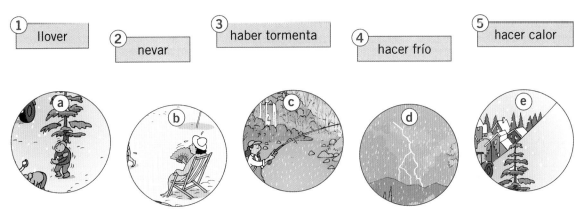

3 Fill in the missing letters to complete the names of these outdoor activities.

1 __c__mp__r

2 t__m__r __l s__l

3 p__sca__

4 h__c__r s__n__eris__o

5 m__nt__r __ c__b__ll__

6 h__c__r b__c____

7 __squ____r

8 __sc__lar

1 Fill in the missing letters to complete the names of the months of the year.

1 __n__r__

2 f_e_br_e_r_o

3 m_a_rz_o

4 _a_br_i_l

5 m_a_y_o

6 j_u_n_i_o

7 j_u_l_i_o

8 _a_g_o_st_o

9 s_e_pti_e_mbr_e

10 _o_ct_u_br_e

11 n_o_v_i_e_mbr_e

12 d_i_c_i_e_mbr_e

2 Put the names of the week that are missing on the list.

| el domingo | el martes | el sábado | el viernes | el miércoles |

1 el lunes

2 el martes

3 el miércoles

4 el jueves

5 el viernes

6 el sabado

7 el domingo

3 Look at the watches and complete the times.

1 _____ la una
en _punto_

2 _____ un cuarto
_____ las siete.

3 Son las cuatro _____
cinco.

4 Son las cinco
y _____.

5 Son las seis
y _____.

6 Son las _____
de la mañana.

1 What color is it? Write the name of the corresponding color.

| azul | blanco | verde | amarillo | rojo | negro | café | anaranjado |

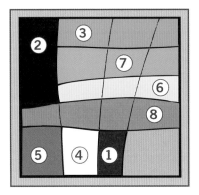

1 _____ 2 _____ 3 _____ 4 _____

5 _____ 6 _____ 7 _____ 8 _____

2 Write the name of these numbers.

a 15 _____   b 6 _____   c 12 _____

d 18 _____   e 10 _____   f 14 _____

g 1,30 _____   h 20 _____   i 50 _____

j 100 _____   k 1000 _____ l 1 000 000 _____

3 Mark the words that are illustrated in the pictures.

☐ estar viejo   ☐ estar grande   ☐ ser redondo
☐ estar nuevo   ☐ estar pequeño   ☐ ser cuadrado

4 Write the ordinal numbers that are missing from this list.

1.º primero   2.º _____   3.º tercero   4.º _____   5.º quinto

6.º _____   7.º séptimo   8.º _____   9.º noveno   10.º _____

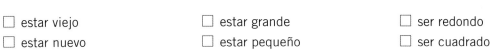

Soluciones: 1. 1 rojo; 2 negro; 3 azul; 4 blanco; 5 café; 6 amarillo; 7 verde; 8 anaranjado.
2. a quince; b seis; c doce; d dieciocho; e diez; f catorce; g uno con treinta; h veinte;
i cincuenta; j cien; k mil; l un millón.
3. 1 estar nuevo; 2 estar grande; 3 ser cuadrado.
4. 2.º segundo; 4.º cuarto; 6.º sexto; 8.º octavo; 10.º décimo.

1 Write the name of these parts of the car.

1 el _____

2 los _____

3 la _____

4 el _____

5 el _____

6 el _____

7 la _____

8 el _____

9 la _____

10 la _____

11 el _____

12 la _____

13 el _____

14 el _____

15 el _____

16 el _____

2 Look at the pictures and complete the crossword puzzle.

1 Unscramble the letters. Then match the words with the pictures.

1 la nociafi de moturis

_____

2 la jetarta ed baremque

_____

3 el tobelo ed vianó

_____

4 la lamochi

_____

5 el viaón

_____

6 la fazataa

_____

2 First put these actions in the right order. Then write each action below the matching picture.

_____ deshacer las maletas

_1.°_ hacer las maletas

_____ recoger el equipaje

_____ facturar el equipaje

_____ volar

_____ aterrizar

_____ despedirse

_____ despegar

a _____

b _____

c _____

d _____

e _____

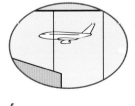

f _____

g _____

h _____

1 Look at the pictures. Then write the right verb under each picture.
Be careful! There are more words than pictures!

depositar dinero	sacar dinero	ayudar	recibir una carta

abrir una carta	enviar un paquete

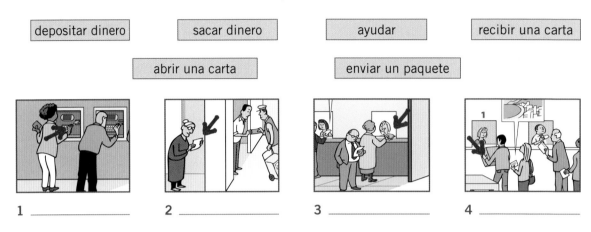

1 _____   2 _____   3 _____   4 _____

2 Fill in the word map with the missing words.

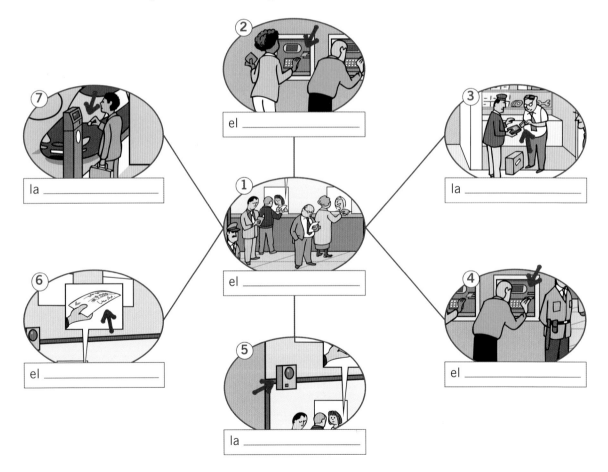

el _____

la _____

la _____

el _____

el _____

el _____

la _____

1 Look at the pictures and write the name of each animal underneath. Then match each one to a verb.

1 el _____

2 el _____

3 el _maulla_

4 la _mugir_

5 la _Cacarear_

6 el _relinchar_

7 la _____

8 el _____

9 la _Croar_

10 el _rugir_

a maullar

b ladrar

c mugir

d picar

e cacarear

f piar

g croar

h balar

i rugir

j relinchar

Soluciones: 1. 1 el mosquito-d; 2 el gato-a; 3 el perro-b;
4 la vaca-c; 5 la gallina-e; 6 el caballo-j; 7 la oveja-h; 8 el pájaro-f;
9 la rana-g; 10 el león-i.

1 Write the name of the corresponding country or nationality.

1 Los Estados Unidos: _____

2 _____: canadiense

3 China: _____

4 _____: japonés

5 Australia: _____

6 _____: francés

7 Alemania: _____

8 _____: italiano

9 Grecia: _____

10 _____: mexicano

11 España: _____

12 _____: salvadoreño

13 República Dominicana: _____

14 _____: costarricense

15 Colombia: _____

16 _____: boliviano

17 Argentina: _____

18 _____: chileno

2 Match each country with its capital.

| 1 Bolivia | 3 Colombia | 5 Uruguay | 7 Costa Rica | 9 Reino Unido |

| 2 Cuba | 4 Venezuela | 6 Chile | 8 Argentina | 10 España |

| a Santiago | c San José | e Madrid | g Buenos Aires | i La Paz |

| b Montevideo | d Caracas | f Londres | h Bogotá | j La Habana |

3 Look in the word search for the names of the continents.

D	R	T	G	H	Y	U	J	K	I	H	F	C
P	O	C	P	O	C	E	A	N	Í	A	O	V
U	J	K	I	H	F	C	M	A	D	E	E	Á
E	Y	A	M	B	U	L	É	N	C	I	A	F
V	I	G	A	N	T	Á	R	T	I	D	A	R
H	E	T	T	T	E	E	I	R	D	E	T	I
R	A	R	F	I	N	R	C	E	R	T	Y	C
S	S	D	C	S	F	M	A	D	T	A	H	A
A	I	S	O	T	E	E	I	C	T	O	N	T
A	A	Z	B	A	E	U	R	O	P	A	M	A
R	T	G	H	Y	U	A	F	X	N	M	J	L

Spanish-English Glossary

abajo (estar ~): below (to be ~) U7, p. 20
abeja (f.): bee U23, p. 53
abierto (estar ~): open (to be ~) U7, p. 21
abogado (m.): lawyer U5, p. 16
abrigo (m.): coat U4, p. 15
abril: April U18, p. 42
abrir una carta: to open a letter U22, p. 50
abrocharse: to button (up), to fasten U4, p. 14
abuela (f.): grandmother U1, p. 9
abuelo (m.): grandfather U1, p. 9
abuelos (m.): grandparents U1, p. 9
aburrido (estar ~): bored (to be ~) U3, p. 13
aburrirse: to get bored U15, p. 36
acá (estar ~): here (to be ~) U7, p. 20
acampar: to camp, to go camping U17, p. 41
aceite (m.): oil U13, p. 33
acelerar: to accelerate U20, p. 46
acelga (f.): Swiss chard U12, p. 30
acera (f.): sidewalk U9, p. 24
acostado (estar ~): lying down (to be ~) U6, p. 19
acostarse: to go to bed U1, p. 9
acotamiento (m.): shoulder U20, p. 46
actor (m.): actor U5, p. 16
actriz (f.): actress U5, p. 16
adelantar: to pass U20, p. 46
adentro (estar ~): inside (to be ~) U7, p. 20
adolescente (m./f.): adolescent, teenager U2, p. 10
aduana (f.): Customs U21, p. 48
adulto (m.): adult U2, p. 10
aeropuerto (m.): airport U21, p. 48
afeitarse: to shave U1, p. 9
África: Africa U24, p. 56
afuera (estar ~): outside (to be ~) U7, p. 20
afueras (f.): the outskirts U9, p. 24
agencia de viajes (f.): travel agency U10, p. 27
agenda (f.): calendar U14, p. 35
agosto: August U18, p. 42
agricultor (m.): farmer U5, p. 16
agua (f.): water U13, p. 33
aguacate (m.): avocado U12, p. 31
águila (f.): eagle U23, p. 53
aire acondicionado (m.): air conditioning U7, p. 21
ajo (m.): garlic U12, p. 30
ala (f.): wing U21, p. 49
alarma (f.): alarm U22, p. 51
albañil (m.): bricklayer U5, p. 17
alcachofa (f.): artichoke U12, p. 30
alcalde (m.): mayor U5, p. 16
alcantarilla (f.): sewer U9, p. 25
alegre (ser ~): happy (to be ~) U3, p. 12
alemán: German U24, p. 56
Alemania: Germany U24, p. 56
alfombra (f.): rug U8, p. 23
allá (estar ~): over there (to be ~) U7, p. 20
allí (estar ~): there (to be ~) U7, p. 20
almendra (f.): almond U12, p. 31
almohada (f.): pillow U8, p. 23
almorzar: to have lunch U13, p. 32
alquilar: to rent U7, p. 21
alto (ser ~): tall (to be ~) U2, p. 10
ama de casa (f.): housewife U5, p. 17
amable (ser ~): kind (to be ~), nice (to be ~) U3, p. 12
amanecer: to get light U18, p. 43
amarillo (ser ~): yellow (to be ~) U19, p. 45

ambulancia (f.): ambulance U6, p. 18
América del Norte: North America U24, p. 56
~ **del Sur**: South America U24, p. 56
amigo (m.): friend U1, p. 8
anaranjado (ser ~): orange (to be ~) U19, p. 45
ancho (estar ~): loose (to be ~) U4, p. 14
anciano (m.): elderly person, old man U2, p. 10
andén (m.): platform U9, p. 25
anillo (m.): ring U4, p. 15
año (m.): year U18, p. 42
Año Nuevo (m.): New Year's Day U18, p. 42
Antártida: Antarctica U24, p. 56
antena (f.): antenna U7, p. 21
antes de ayer: the day before yesterday U18, p. 43
antipático (ser ~): unfriendly (to be ~) U3, p. 12
apagar: to turn off U14, p. 34
~ **un incendio**: to put out a fire U22, p. 51
apartamento (m.): apartment U7, p. 20
apellido (m.): last name U22, p. 51
apio (m.): celery U12, p. 30
aplaudir: to applaud, to clap U15, p. 36
aquí (estar ~): here (to be ~) U7, p. 20
árabe: Arabic U24, p. 56
arándano (m.): blueberry U12, p. 31
árbitro (m.): referee U16, p. 39
árbol (m.): tree U17, p. 41
arcen (m.): shoulder U20, p. 46
archivar: to file U14, p. 35
arco (m.): goal U16, p. 39
área de servicio (m.): service station U20, p. 46
arena (f.): sand U17, p. 41
aretes (m.): earrings U4, p. 15
Argentina: Argentina U24, p. 56
argentino: Argentinian U24, p. 56
armario (m.): closet U8, p. 23
arquero (m.): goalkeeper U16, p. 39
arquitecto (m.): architect U5, p. 17
arrancar: to start (up) U20, p. 46
arriba (estar ~): above (to be ~), on top of (to be ~) U7, p. 20
arroba (f.): "at" symbol U14, p. 35
arroz (m.): rice U11, p. 29
artículos de limpieza (m.): cleaning products U11, p. 28
arveja (f.): pea U12, p. 30
ascensor (m.): elevator U7, p. 21
Asia: Asia U24, p. 56
asiento (m.): seat U20, p. 47
atardecer: to get dark U18, p. 43
atasco (m.): traffic jam U20, p. 47
aterrizar: to land U21, p. 48
atletismo (m.): track and field U16, p. 38
atrás (estar ~): behind (to be ~) U7, p. 20
Australia: Australia U24, p. 56
australiano: Australian U24, p. 56
Austria: Austria U24, p. 56
austriaco: Austrian U24, p. 56
auto (m.): car U9, p. 25
autobús (m.): bus U9, p. 25
autopista (f.): freeway U20, p. 46
auxiliar de vuelo (m.): flight attendant U21, p. 48
avellana (f.): hazelnut U12, p. 31
avenida (f.): avenue U9, p. 24
averiarse: to break down U20, p. 47
avión (m.): airplane U21, p. 49
ayer: yesterday U18, p. 43
ayudar: to help U22, p. 51

azafata (f.): flight attendant U21, p. 48
azucarera (f.): sugar bowl U13, p. 33
azucarero (m.): sugar bowl U13, p. 33
azul (ser ~): blue (to be ~) U19, p. 45

b

bailar: to dance U15, p. 36
bailarín (m.): dancer U15, p. 36
bajar del autobús: to get off a bus U9, p. 25
bajo (ser ~): short (to be ~) U2, p. 10
balancín (m.): seesaw U15, p. 37
balar: to bleat U23, p. 52
ballena (f.): whale U23, p. 53
bañarse: to take a bath U1, p. 9
banco (m.): bench U9, p. 25; bank U22, p. 50
bandeja (f.): tray U13, p. 32
bañera (f.): bathtub U8, p. 23
(cuarto de) baño (m.): bathroom U8, p. 22
barato (ser ~): cheap (to be ~) U11, p. 28
barco de vela (m.): sailboat U17, p. 41
barra de chocolate (f.): chocolate bar U11, p. 29
   ~ de pan (f.): loaf of bread U11, p. 29
barrendero (m.): street cleaner U5, p. 16
barrio (m.): neighborhood U9, p. 24
basquetbol, básquetbol (m.): basketball U16, p. 38
bate (m.): bat U16, p. 39
batería (f.): battery U20, p. 47
bebé (m.): baby U2, p. 10
beber: to drink U13, p. 32
bebidas (f.): drinks U11, p. 28
béisbol (m.): baseball U16, p. 38
belga: Belgian U24, p. 56
Bélgica: Belgium U24, p. 56
bengalí: Bengali U24, p. 56
berenjena (f.): eggplant U12, p. 30
besar: to kiss U3, p. 13
biblioteca (f.): library U9, p. 24
bicicleta (f.): bicycle U16, p. 38
bikini (m.): bikini U4, p. 15
billete (m.): bill U22, p. 50
billetera (f.): wallet U22, p. 50
bistec con papas (m.): steak with potatoes U13, p. 33
blanco (ser ~): white (to be ~) U19, p. 45
blusa (f.): blouse U4, p. 15
boca (f.): mouth U6, p. 19
bocina (f.): horn U20, p. 47
boda (f.): wedding U1, p. 8
bol (m.): bowl U13, p. 33
boletería (f.): box office U15, p. 37
boleto (m.): ticket U15, p. 37
   ~ (de avión) (m.): plane ticket U21, p. 48
bolígrafo (m.): pen U14, p. 35
Bolivia: Bolivia U24, p. 56
boliviano: Bolivian U24, p. 56
bolsa (f.): purse U4, p. 15; bag U10, p. 26
bolso (m.): purse U4, p. 15
bombero (m.): fireman U22, p. 51
bonito (ser ~): nice (to be ~), pretty (to be ~) U4, p. 14
bosque (m.): forest U17, p. 40
botas (f.): boots U4, p. 15
bote de basura (m.): garbage can U7, p. 21; trash can U9, p. 25
botella (f.): bottle U11, p. 29
bragas (f.): panties U4, p. 15

Brasil: Brazil U24, p. 56
brasileño: Brazilian U24, p. 56
brazo (m.): arm U6, p. 19
británico: British U24, p. 56
brócoli (m.): broccoli U12, p. 30
bronceado (estar ~): tan (to be ~), dark skin (to have ~) U2, p. 11
bucear: to go scuba diving U17, p. 41
bufanda (f.): scarf U4, p. 15
bufete (m.): law firm U5, p. 17
butaca (f.): seat U15, p. 37
buzón (m.): mailbox U9, p. 25

c

caballo (m.): horse U23, p. 52
cabeza (f.): head U6, p. 19
cabina telefónica (f.): telephone booth U9, p. 25
cacahuate (m.): peanut U12, p. 31
cacarear: to crow, to cluck U23, p. 52
cachete (m.): cheek U6, p. 19
café (m.): coffee U13, p. 33
   ~ con leche (m.): coffee with milk U13, p. 33
   ~ (ser ~): brown (to be ~) U19, p. 45
cafetera (f.): coffee pot U13, p. 33
cafetería (f.): café U15, p. 36
caja (f.): checkout U11, p. 28; box U11, p. 29
   ~ de cambios (f.): stick shift U20, p. 47
   ~ de velocidades (f.): stick shift U20, p. 47
cajero (m.): cashier U11, p. 28
   ~ automático (m.): automated teller machine (ATM) U22, p. 50
cajuela (f.): trunk U20, p. 47
calabaza (f.): pumpkin U12, p. 30
calcetines (m.): socks U4, p. 15
calculadora (f.): calculator U14, p. 35
calefacción (f.): heating U7, p. 21
calendario (m.): calendar U18, p. 42
caliente (estar ~): hot (to be ~) U13, p. 32
calle (f.): street U9, p. 24
calvo (estar ~): bald (to be ~) U2, p. 11
calzoncillos (m.): underpants U4, p. 15
calzones (m.): panties U4, p. 15
cama (f.): bed U8, p. 23
   ~ matrimonial (f.): double bed U8, p. 23
cámara de fotos (f.): camera U15, p. 36
   ~ fotográfica (f.): camera U15, p. 36
camarero (m.): waiter U13, p. 32
cambiar: to exchange U10, p. 26
   ~ dinero: to exchange money U21, p. 49
camión (m.): truck U20, p. 46
   ~ de bomberos (m.): fire truck U22, p. 51
camionero (m.): truck driver U5, p. 16
camioneta (f.): van U20, p. 46
camisa (f.): shirt U4, p. 15
camiseta (f.): T-shirt U16, p. 38
campo (m.): countryside U17, p. 40
   ~ de fútbol (m.): football field U16, p. 39
caña de pescar (f.): fishing rod U17, p. 41
Canadá: Canada U24, p. 56
canadiense: Canadian U24, p. 56
canasta (f.): basket U16, p. 39
cancha (f.): field U16, p. 39
   ~ de tenis (f.): tennis court U16, p. 39
cansado (estar ~): tired (to be ~) U3, p. 13

cantante (m./f.): singer U15, p. 37
cantar: to sing U15, p. 37
cantimplora (f.): canteen U17, p. 41
capital (f.): capital (city) U21, p. 48
capó (m.): hood U20, p. 47
caracol (m.): snail U23, p. 53
cariñoso (ser ~): affectionate (to be ~) U3, p. 13
carne (f.): meat U11, p. 29
  ~ de res (f.): beef U11, p. 29
carnicería (f.): butcher shop U11, p. 29
carnicero (m.): butcher U11, p. 29
carnívoro (ser ~): carnivorous (to be ~),
  meat-eating U23, p. 52
caro (ser ~): expensive (to be ~) U11, p. 28
carpa (f.): tent U17, p. 41
carpeta (f.): folder U14, p. 35
carpintero (m.): carpenter U5, p. 17
carretera (f.): highway U20, p. 46
carril (m.): lane U20, p. 46
carrito (m.): cart U21, p. 49
carro (m.): shopping cart U11, p. 28
carrusel (m.): merry-go-round, carousel U15, p. 37
carta (f.): letter U22, p. 51
cartero (m.): mailman U22, p. 50
cartilla (f.): passbook U22, p. 51
casa (f.): house U7, p. 20
casado (estar/ser ~): married (to be ~) U1, p. 8
cascada (f.): waterfall U17, p. 41
casco (m.): helmet U16, p. 38
catorce: fourteen U19, p. 44
cebolla (f.): onion U12, p. 30
cebra (f.): zebra U23, p. 53
cejas (f.): eyebrows U6, p. 19
(teléfono) celular (m.): cell phone U14, p. 35
cenar: to have dinner, to have supper U13, p. 32
centro (de la ciudad) (m.): downtown U9, p. 24
(en el) centro (estar ~): in the middle (to be ~),
  in the center (to be ~) U7, p. 20
centro comercial (m.): shopping center, shopping
  mall U10, p. 26
cepillo de dientes (m.): toothbrush U8, p. 23
cerca (estar ~): near (to be ~) U7, p. 20
cerdo (m.): pork U11, p. 29; pig U23, p. 52
cereales (m.): cereal U13, p. 33
cereza (f.): cherry U12, p. 31
cero con veinte: zero point twenty U19, p. 45
cerrado (estar ~): closed (to be ~) U7, p. 21
cerrar una carta: to seal a letter U22, p. 50
chaleco salvavidas (m.): life vest U17, p. 41
champú (m.): shampoo U8, p. 23
chaqueta (f.): jacket U4, p. 15
cheque (m.): check U22, p. 51
Chile: Chile U24, p. 56
chileno: Chilean U24, p. 56
chimenea (f.): chimney U7, p. 21
China: China U24, p. 56
chino: Chinese U24, p. 56
chocar: to crash U20, p. 47
chofer (m.): bus driver U5, p. 16
choque (m.): crash, accident U20, p. 47
ciclismo (m.): cycling U16, p. 38
ciego (estar ~): blind (to be ~), sight impaired U2, p. 10
cielo (m.): sky U17, p. 40
cien: a hundred U19, p. 45
científico (m.): scientist U5, p. 17
cinco: five U19, p. 44

cincuenta: fifty U19, p. 45
cine (m.): movie theater U15, p. 37
cinta adhesiva (f.): Scotch tape®, tape U14, p. 35
cinturón (m.): belt U4, p. 14
  ~ de seguridad (m.): seat belt U20, p. 47
cirujano (m.): surgeon U6, p. 18
clavado (m.): to dive U16, p. 39
claxon (m.): horn U20, p. 47
cliente (m.): customer U10, p. 26
clínica veterinaria (f.): veterinary clinic U5, p. 17
clip (m.): paper clip U14, p. 35
cocina (f.): kitchen U8, p. 22; electric stove U8, p. 23
cocinar: to cook U13, p. 32
cocinero (m.): chef, cook U13, p. 32
cocodrilo (m.): crocodile U23, p. 53
código postal (m.): ZIP code U22, p. 51
codo (m.): elbow U6, p. 19
col (f.): cabbage U12, p. 30
cola (f.): tail U21, p. 49, U23, p. 53
coliflor (f.): cauliflower U12, p. 30
collar (m.): necklace U4, p. 15
Colombia: Colombia U24, p. 56
colombiano: Colombian U24, p. 56
columpio (m.): swing U15, p. 37
comedor (m.): dining room U8, p. 22
comer: to eat U13, p. 32
cometa (f.): kite U15, p. 37
comisaría (f.): police station U22, p. 51
compañero (m.): coworker U14, p. 34
compañía aérea (f.): airline U21, p. 49
comprar: to buy U10, p. 26
computadora (f.): desktop computer U14, p. 35
  ~ portátil (f.): laptop computer U14, p. 35
concierto (m.): concert U15, p. 37
conducir: to drive U20, p. 46
conejo (m.): rabbit U23, p. 53
congelados (m.): frozen foods U11, p. 28
conservas (f.): canned goods U11, p. 28
consulta del psicólogo (f.): psychologist's office U5, p. 17
consultar un mapa: to check a map U21, p. 49
consultorio (m.): psychologist's office U5, p. 17
contenedor de basura (m.): garbage can U7, p. 21
contento (estar ~): happy (to be ~) U3, p. 12
contestar: to answer U9, p. 25
contratar a alguien: to hire someone U14, p. 35
convertible (m.): convertible U20, p. 46
copa (f.): wine glass U13, p. 33
corbata (f.): tie U4, p. 14
coreano (m.): Korean U24, p. 56
correo certificado (m.): certified mail U22, p. 50
  ~ urgente (m.): priority mail U22, p. 50
correr: to run U16, p. 38
cortar: to cut U11, p. 28
cortinas (f.): curtains U8, p. 23
corto (estar ~): short (to be ~) U4, p. 14
Costa Rica: Costa Rica U24, p. 56
costar: to cost U11, p. 28
costarricense: Costa Rican U24, p. 56
CPU (f.): CPU U14, p. 35
croar: to croak U23, p. 52
cruce peatonal (m.): crosswalk U9, p. 25
cruzar la calle: to cross U9, p. 25
cuaderno (m.): notebook U14, p. 35
cuadra (f.): block U9, p. 24
cuadrado (ser ~): square (to be ~) U19, p. 44
cuadro (m.): painting U15, p. 37

cuarenta: forty U19, p. 45
cuarto: fourth, quarter U19, p. 45
cuatro: four U19, p. 44
Cuba: Cuba U24, p. 56
cubano: Cuban U24, p. 56
cuchara (f.): spoon U13, p. 33
cucharita (f.): teaspoon U13, p. 33
cuchillo (m.): knife U13, p. 33
cuello (m.): neck U6, p. 19
cuñado (m.): brother-in-law U1, p. 8
currículum (m.): résumé, curriculum vitae U14, p. 35
curva (f.): curve U20, p. 46

d

danés: Danish U24, p. 56
dar asco: to disgust, to gross out U3, p. 13
   ~ vergüenza: to be embarrassed U3, p. 13
   ~ vuelta a la derecha: to turn right U9, p. 24
   ~ vuelta a la izquierda: to turn left U9, p. 24
dátil (m.): date U12, p. 31
debajo (estar ~): under (to be ~) U7, p. 20
décimo: tenth U19, p. 45
decorado (m.): scenery U15, p. 37
dedo anular (m.): ring finger U6, p. 19
   ~ corazón (m.): middle finger U6, p. 19
   ~ índice (m.): index finger U6, p. 19
   ~ meñique (m.): little finger U6, p. 19
   ~ pulgar (m.): thumb U6, p. 19
defensas (f.): bumper U20, p. 47
dejar un recado: to leave a message U14, p. 34
   ~ una propina: to leave a tip U13, p. 32
delante (estar ~): in front of (to be ~) U7, p. 20
delfín (m.): dolphin U23, p. 53
delgado (ser ~): thin (to be ~) U2, p. 10
delicioso (estar ~): good (to be ~), delicious (to be ~) U13, p. 32
dentista (m./f.): dentist U6, p. 18
depositar dinero: to deposit money U22, p. 51
desabrocharse: to unbutton, to unfasten U4, p. 14
desayunar: to have breakfast U13, p. 32
descansar: to rest U16, p. 38
descapotable (m.): convertible U20, p. 46
descomponerse: to break down U20, p. 47
desempleado (estar ~): unemployed (to be ~) U5, p. 16
deshacer las maletas: to unpack (suitcases, bags) U21, p. 49
desordenado (ser ~): messy (to be ~) U3, p. 13
despacho (m.): office U8, p. 22, U14, p. 34
despedirse: to say good-bye U21, p. 48
despegar: to take off U21, p. 48
despertador (m.): alarm clock U8, p. 23
despistado (ser ~): absentminded (to be ~), U3, p. 13
destinatario (m.): addressee U22, p. 51
destino (m.): destination U21, p. 49
detener: to arrest U22, p. 51
detrás (estar ~): behind (to be ~) U7, p. 20
devolver: to throw up, to vomit U6, p. 18; to return U10, p. 26
día (m.): day U18, p. 42
   ~ feriado (m.): holiday U18, p. 42
diciembre: December U18, p. 42
diecinueve: nineteen U19, p. 45
dieciocho: eighteen U19, p. 45
dieciséis: sixteen U19, p. 45
diecisiete: seventeen U19, p. 45

diente (m.): tooth U6, p. 19
diésel (m.): diesel (fuel) U20, p. 47
diez: ten U19, p. 44
Dinamarca: Denmark U24, p. 56
dinero (m.): money U22, p. 50
dirección (f.): address U22, p. 51
direccional (m.): turn signal U20, p. 47
director (m.): manager U14, p. 34; conductor U15, p. 37
directorio (m.): directory U10, p. 26
divertirse: to have fun U15, p. 36
divorciado (estar/ser ~): divorced (to be ~) U1, p. 8
doce: twelve U19, p. 44
docena de huevos (f.): dozen eggs U11, p. 29
doler la cabeza: to have a headache U6, p. 18
domingo (m.): Sunday U18, p. 43
dominicano: Dominican U24, p. 56
dormir: to sleep U1, p. 9
dos: two U19, p. 44
ducha (f.): shower U8, p. 23
ducharse: to take a shower U1, p. 9
durazno (m.): peach U12, p. 31
(reproductor de) DVD (m.): DVD (player) U8, p. 23

e

echar de menos: to miss U3, p. 13
Ecuador: Ecuador U24, p. 56
ecuatoriano: Ecuadorian U24, p. 56
edificio (m.): building U7, p. 20
   ~ de apartamentos (m.): apartment building U9, p. 24
edredón (m.): comforter U8, p. 23
educado (ser ~): polite (to be ~), well-mannered (to be ~) U3, p. 13
egipcio: Egyptian U24, p. 56
Egipto: Egypt U24, p. 56
egoísta (ser ~): selfish (to be ~) U3, p. 12
ejecutivo (m.): executive U5, p. 17
El Salvador: El Salvador U24, p. 56
electricista (m.): electrician U5, p. 17
elefante (m.): elephant U23, p. 53
elevador (m.): elevator U7, p. 21
embarazada (estar ~): pregnant (to be ~) U2, p. 10
embarcar: to board U21, p. 48
embotellamiento (m.): traffic jam U20, p. 47
embutidos (m.): cold cuts U11, p. 29
empatar: to tie (in a game or contest) U16, p. 38
empleada doméstica (f.): cleaning lady, domestic worker U5, p. 17
empleado (m.): employee U14, p. 34
empresa (f.): company U14, p. 34
empresario (m.): business man U5, p. 17
empujar: to push U20, p. 47
enamorado (estar ~): in love (to be ~) U3, p. 13
encender: to turn on U14, p. 35
enchufe (m.): socket U8, p. 22
encima (estar ~): on top of (to be ~) U7, p. 20
enero: January U18, p. 42
enfermero (m.): nurse U6, p. 18
enfermo (estar ~): sick (to be ~) U6, p. 18
enfrente (estar ~): in front of (to be ~) U7, p. 20
engrapadora (f.): stapler U14, p. 35
enojado (estar ~): angry (to be ~) U3, p. 13
ensalada (f.): salad U13, p. 33
entrada (f.): entrance U10, p. 27; first course U13, p. 33
entrar: to come in, to go in U9, p. 24
entre (estar ~): between (to be ~) U7, p. 20

entregar un **telegrama**: to deliver a telegram
U22, p. 50
entrenador (m.): coach U16, p. 39
entrevista (f.): interview U14, p. 35
envase de cartón (m.): carton U11, p. 29
enviar un fax: to send a fax U14, p. 34
~ **un paquete**: to send a package U22, p. 50
envidioso (ser ~): envious (to be ~), jealous (to be ~)
U3, p. 13
enyesado (estar ~): in a cast (to be ~) U6, p. 18
equipaje (m.): baggage, luggage U21, p. 49
equipo (m.): team U16, p. 39
es la una en punto: it's exactly one o'clock U18, p. 43
escalar: to climb U17, p. 41
escalera (f.): stairway U7, p. 21
escaleras eléctricas (f.): escalator U10, p. 26
~ **mecánicas** (f.): escalator U10, p. 26
escaparate (m.): window display U10, p. 26
escenario (m.): stage U15, p. 37
escenografía (f.): scenery U15, p. 37
escribir un correo electrónico: to email U14, p. 35
escritor (m.): writer U5, p. 17
escritorio (m.): desk U8, p. 23
escuchar música: to listen to music U15, p. 37
escuela (f.): school U9, p. 24
escultura (f.): sculpture U15, p. 37
espalda (f.): back U6, p. 19
España. Spain U24, p. 56
español: Spanish U24, p. 56
espárrago (m.): asparagus U12, p. 30
espejo (m.): mirror U8, p. 22
esperar: to wait U21, p. 48
espinaca (f.): spinach U12, p. 30
esponja (f.): sponge U8, p. 23
esposa (f.): wife U1, p. 8
esposo (m.): husband U1, p. 8
esquiar: to ski, to go skiing U17, p. 41
esquina (f.): corner U9, p. 24
establo (m.): stable U17, p. 41
estación de metro (f.): subway station U9, p. 25
~ **de tren** (f.): train station U9, p. 25
estacionamiento (m.): parking lot U9, p. 25
estacionarse: to park U20, p. 46
estado de cuenta (m.): statement U22, p. 51
(los) Estados Unidos: the United States
of America U24, p. 56
estadounidense: American U24, p. 56
estantería (f.): bookshelf U8, p. 23
Este: East U24, p. 56
estómago (m.): stomach U6, p. 19
estornudar: to sneeze U6, p. 18
estrecho (estar ~): tight (to be ~) U4, p. 14
estrella (f.): star U17, p. 40
~ **de mar** (f.): starfish U23, p. 53
estudiante (m.): student U5, p. 17
estudiar: to study U5, p. 17
estudio (m.): studio apartment U7, p. 20
~ **de arquitectura** (m.): architect's studio
U5, p. 17
estufa (f.): electric stove U8, p. 23
etiqueta (f.): tag U10, p. 26
Europa: Europe U24, p. 56
exposición (f.): exhibition U15, p. 37
extracto (m.): statement U22, p. 51
extrañar: to miss U3, p. 13

fábrica (f.): factory U5, p. 17
facturar el equipaje: to check in luggage U21, p. 49
falda (f.): skirt U4, p. 15
falta un cuarto para las siete: it's quarter
of seven, it's quarter till seven U18, p. 43
faltan diez para las ocho: it's ten of eight U18, p. 43
farmacéutico (m.): pharmacist U10, p. 27
farmacia (f.): pharmacy U10, p. 27
farol (m.): streetlight U9, p. 25
farola (f.): streetlight U9, p. 25
fax (m.): fax U14, p. 34
febrero: February U18, p. 42
fecha (f.): date U18, p. 42
feo (ser ~): ugly (to be ~) U4, p. 14
fiambres (m.): cold cuts U11, p. 29
fiesta de cumpleaños (f.): birthday party U1, p. 8
fin de semana (m.): weekend U18, p. 43
firmar: to sign U14, p. 34
flojo (ser ~): lazy (to be ~) U3, p. 12
flor (f.): flower U10, p. 27
florería (f.): florist U10, p. 27
floristería (f.): florist U10, p. 27
flotador (m.): float ring U17, p. 41
foca (f.): seal U23, p. 53
fotocopiadora (f.): photocopier U14, p. 35
fotocopiar: to photocopy, to make photocopies U14, p. 35
fotógrafo (m.): photographer U5, p. 16
frambuesa (f.): raspberry U12, p. 31
francés: French U24, p. 56
Francia: France U24, p. 56
fregadero (m.): sink U8, p. 23
frenar: to brake, to stop U20, p. 46
frente (f.): forehead U6, p. 19
fresa (f.): strawberry U12, p. 31
frijol (m.): bean U12, p. 31
frío (estar ~): cold (to be ~) U13, p. 32
fruta (f.): fruit U11, p. 29
frutería (f.): fruit shop U11, p. 29
frutero (m.): fruit seller U11, p. 29
fuente (f.): fountain U9, p. 25
fuerte (ser ~): strong (to be ~) U2, p. 10
funcionario (m.): civil servant U5, p. 16
furgoneta (f.): van U20, p. 46
fútbol (m.): soccer U16, p. 38
~ **americano** (m.): football U16, p. 38

gafas (f.): goggles U16, p. 39
~ **de sol** (f.): sunglasses U4, p. 15
galleta (f.): cookie U11, p. 29
gallina (f.): hen U23, p. 52
ganar: to win U16, p. 38
gancho (m.): hanger U4, p. 14
garaje (m.): garage U7, p. 21
garbanzo (m.): chickpea U12, p. 31
garganta (f.): throat U6, p. 19
gasoil (m.): diesel (fuel) U20, p. 47
gasolina (f.): gas U20, p. 47
gasolinera (f.): gas station U20, p. 47
gato (m.): jack U20, p. 47; cat U23, p. 52
gel (m.): liquid soap, shower gel U8, p. 23
gemelos (m.): twins U1, p. 8

generoso (ser ~): generous (to be ~) U3, p. 12
gerente (m.): manager U14, p. 34
gimnasio (m.): gym, gymnasium U16, p. 39
girar a la derecha: to turn right U9, p. 24
 ~ a la izquierda: to turn left U9, p. 24
golf (m.): golf U16, p. 38
goma de borrar (f.): eraser U14, p. 35
gordo (ser ~): fat (to be ~) U2, p. 10
gorra (f.): cap U16, p. 39
gorro (m.): swim cap U16, p. 39
gracioso (ser ~): funny (to be ~) U3, p. 12
grande (estar/ser ~): large (to be ~), big (to be ~) U19, p. 44
grapadora (f.): stapler U14, p. 35
Grecia: Greece U24, p. 56
griego: Greek U24, p. 56
grifo (m.): faucet U8, p. 23
gris (ser ~): gray (to be ~) U19, p. 45
grúa (f.): tow truck U20, p. 47
guante de béisbol (m.): baseball glove U16, p. 39
guantera (f.): glove compartment U20, p. 47
guantes (m.): gloves U4, p. 15
guapo (ser ~): good-looking (to be ~) U2, p. 10
guardia de seguridad (m./f.): security guard U22, p. 51
Guatemala: Guatemala U24, p. 56
guatemalteco: Guatemalan U24, p. 56
guía turístico (m./f.): tour guide U21, p. 49
guitarra (f.): guitar U15, p. 37
gustar: to like U3, p. 13

h

haber niebla: to be foggy U17, p. 40
 ~ tormenta: there´s a storm, to be stormy U17, p. 40
habichuela (f.): green bean U12, p. 30
habitación (f.): bedroom U8, p. 22
 ~ doble (f.): double room U21, p. 49
 ~ individual (f.): single room U21, p. 49
hablador (ser ~): talkative (to be ~) U3, p. 13
hablar: to talk U1, p. 9
hacer buceo: to go scuba diving U17, p. 41
 ~ calor: to be hot U17, p. 40
 ~ cola: to wait in line U11, p. 28
 ~ ejercicio: to exercise U16, p. 39
 ~ fotocopias: to photocopy U14, p. 35
 ~ frío: to be cold U17, p. 40
 ~ la compra: to go shopping U11, p. 28
 ~ las maletas: to pack (suitcases, bags) U21, p. 49
 ~ senderismo: to hike, to go hiking U17, p. 41
 ~ surf: to surf U17, p. 41
 ~ una reserva: to make a reservation U21, p. 49
 ~ una reservación: to make a reservation U21, p. 49
 ~ viento: to be windy U17, p. 40
Haití: Haiti U24, p. 56
haitiano: Haitian U24, p. 56
harina (f.): flour U11, p. 29
heladería (f.): ice cream parlor U10, p. 27
helado (m.): ice cream U13, p. 33
herbívoro (ser ~): herbivorous (to be ~), grass-eating (to be ~) U23, p. 52
hermana (f.): sister U1, p. 9
hermano (m.): brother U1, p. 9
higo (m.): fig U12, p. 31
hija (f.): daughter U1, p. 9
hijo (m.): son U1, p. 9
 ~ único (m.): only child U1, p. 8

hindi (m.): Hindi U24, p. 56
hipopótamo (m.): hippopotamus U23, p. 53
hocico (m.): snout, muzzle U23, p. 53
hoja (f.): sheet U14, p. 35
holandés: Dutch U24, p. 56
hombre (m.): man U2, p. 10
hombro (m.): shoulder U6, p. 19
Honduras: Honduras U24, p. 56
hondureño: Honduran U24, p. 56
hora (f.): hour U18, p. 42
horno (m.): oven U8, p. 23
hospital (m.): hospital U6, p. 18
hotel (m.): hotel U21, p. 49
hoy: today U18, p. 43

i

iglesia (f.): church U9, p. 24
impaciente (ser ~): impatient (to be ~) U3, p. 13
impresora (f.): printer U14, p. 34
imprimir: to print U14, p. 34
incendio (m.): fire U22, p. 51
India: India U24, p. 56
indio: Indian U24, p. 56
inflar la llanta: to put air in the tire U20, p. 47
infracción (f.): ticket U20, p. 47
ingeniero (m.): engineer U5, p. 16
inglés (m.): English U24, p. 56
inodoro (m.): toilet bowl, toilet U8, p. 23
inteligente (ser ~): intelligent (to be ~) U3, p. 12
intermitente (m.): turn signal U20, p. 47
intérprete (m.): translator, interpreter U5, p. 16
invierno (m.): winter U17, p. 40
invitar: to treat someone, to pay for someone U15, p. 36
ir al cine: to go to the movies U15, p. 37
 ~ al supermercado: to go shopping U11, p. 28
 ~ andando: to walk U9, p. 25
 ~ caminando: to walk U9, p. 25
 ~ de compras: to go shopping U10, p. 26
 ~ en auto: to go by car U9, p. 25
 ~ en canoa: to go canoeing U17, p. 41
 ~ rápido: to go fast, to speed U20, p. 46
Irlanda: Ireland U24, p. 56
irlandés: Irish U24, p. 56
Italia: Italy U24, p. 56
italiano: Italian U24, p. 56

j

jabón (m.): soap U8, p. 23
jamón (m.): ham U11, p. 29
Japón: Japan U24, p. 56
japonés: Japanese U24, p. 56
jardín (m.): yard U7, p. 21
jardinero (m.): gardener U5, p. 16
jarra (f.): pitcher U13, p. 33
javanés: Javanese U24, p. 56
jeans (m.): jeans U4, p. 15
jefe (m.): boss U14, p. 34
jeringa (f.): syringe U6, p. 18
jeringuilla (f.): syringe U6, p. 18
jirafa (f.): giraffe U23, p. 53
joven (ser ~): young (to be ~) U2, p. 10
joyería (f.): jewelry store U10, p. 27
jubilado (estar ~): retired (to be ~) U5, p. 16

jueves (m.): Thursday U18, p. 43
juez (m.): judge U5, p. 16
jugador (m.): player U16, p. 39
jugar a las cartas: to play cards U15, p. 36
   ~a las escondidas: to play hide-and-go-seek U15, p. 36
   ~al ajedrez: to play chess U15, p. 36
   ~al escondite: to play hide-and-go-seek U15, p. 36
   ~al fútbol: to play soccer U16, p. 39
jugo (m.): juice U11, p. 29
juguetería (f.): toy store U10, p. 27
julio: July U18, p. 42
junio: June U18, p. 42

k

kilo (m.): kilo U11, p. 29
kiwi (m.): kiwi U12, p. 31

l

labios (m.): lips U6, p. 19
laboratorio (m.): laboratory, lab U5, p. 17
(al) lado (estar ~): next to (to be ~) U7, p. 20
ladrar: to bark U23, p. 52
lago (m.): lake U17, p. 41
lámpara (f.): desk lamp, lamp U8, p. 23
lanzar (la pelota): to throw (the ball) U16, p. 39
lápiz (m.): pencil U14, p. 35
laptop (m.): laptop computer U14, p. 35
largo (estar ~): long (to be ~) U4, p. 14
lata (f.): can U11, p. 29
lavabo (m.): sink U8, p. 23
lavadora (f.): washing machine U8, p. 23
lavamanos (m.): sink U8, p. 23
lavandería (f.): laundromat U10, p. 27
lavaplatos (m.): dishwasher U8, p. 23
lavar en la lavadora: to do a load of laundry U8, p. 22
   ~los platos: to wash the dishes U8, p. 22
lavarse las manos: to wash one's hands U1, p. 9
   ~los dientes: to brush one's teeth U1, p. 9
leche (f.): milk U11, p. 29
lechuga (f.): lettuce U12, p. 30
leer el periódico: to read the newspaper U1, p. 9
   ~una novela: to read a novel U15, p. 36
lejos (estar ~): far (to be ~) U7, p. 20
lengua (f.): tongue U6, p. 19
lenteja (f.): lentil U12, p. 31
lentes de sol (m.): sunglasses U4, p. 15
león (m.): lion U23, p. 52
levantarse: to get up U1, p. 9
librería (f.): bookstore U10, p. 27
librero (m.): bookshelf U8, p. 23
licencia de conducir (f.): driver's license U20, p. 47
licenciado (ser ~): to have a degree, college graduate
   (to be ~) U5, p. 16
lima, limón (f.): lime U12, p. 31
limón, lima (m.): lemon U12, p. 31
limpiaparabrisas (m.): windshield wipers U20, p. 47
limpiar la casa: to clean the house U8, p. 22
limpio (estar ~): clean (to be ~) U8, p. 22
lindo (ser ~): nice (to be ~), pretty (to be ~) U4, p. 14
linterna (f.): flashlight U17, p. 41
liso (ser ~): plain (to be ~) U4, p. 14
lista de la compra (f.): shopping list U11, p. 28
   ~del supermercado (f.): shopping list U11, p. 28

litro (m.): liter U11, p. 29
llamar por teléfono: to talk on the phone U14, p. 34
llanta (f.): tire, wheel U20, p. 47; hubcap U20, p. 47
llave (f.): faucet U8, p. 23
llegadas (f.): arrivals U21, p. 48
llegar tarde: to arrive late U14, p. 34
llenar el tanque: to fill the tank U20, p. 47
lleno (estar ~): full (to be ~) U3, p. 13, U10, p. 27
llevar fleco: to have bangs U2, p. 11
   ~flequillo: to have bangs U2, p. 11
llorar: to cry U3, p. 13
llover: to rain U17, p. 40
lobo (m.): wolf U23, p. 53
lomo (m.): back U23, p. 53
loro (m.): parrot U23, p. 53
luna (f.): moon U17, p. 40
(a) lunares (ser ~): polka-dotted (to be ~) U4, p. 14
lunes (m.): Monday U18, p. 43
luz (f.): headlight U20, p. 47

m

madre (f.): mother U1, p. 9
maduro (estar ~): ripe (to be ~) U12, p. 31
maíz (m.): corn U12, p. 30
maleducado (ser ~): rude (to be ~), ill-mannered
   (to be ~) U3, p. 13
maleta (f.): suitcase U21, p. 49
maletero (m.): trunk U20, p. 47
maletín (m.): briefcase U14, p. 35
mamá (f.): mother U1, p. 9
mañana: tomorrow U18, p. 43
(en la/por la) mañana: in the morning U18, p. 43
mandarina (f.): mandarin orange, tangerine U12, p. 31
manguera (f.): hose U22, p. 51
maní (m.): peanut U12, p. 31
mano (f.): hand U6, p. 19
manso (ser ~): tame (to be ~), domesticated U23, p. 52
mantel (m.): tablecloth U13, p. 32
mantequilla (f.): butter U13, p. 33
manzana (f.): block U9, p. 24; apple U12, p. 31
mapa (m.): map U21, p. 48
mar (m.): sea U17, p. 41
marcador (m.): scoreboard U16, p. 39
mariposa (f.): butterfly U23, p. 53
marisco (m.): shellfish U11, p. 29
marroquí: Moroccan U24, p. 56
Marruecos: Morocco U24, p. 56
martes (m.): Tuesday U18, p. 43
marzo: March U18, p. 42
matrícula (f.): license plate U20, p. 47
maullar: to mew U23, p. 52
mayo: May U18, p. 42
mayor (ser ~): older (to be ~), old (to be ~) U2, p. 10
mecánico (m.): mechanic U5, p. 17
(a) medianoche: at midnight U18, p. 43
medias (f.): stockings U4, p. 15
medicamento (m.): medicine U6, p. 18
médico (m.): doctor U6, p. 18
(al) mediodía: at noon U18, p. 43
mejilla (f.): cheek U6, p. 19
mellizos (m.): twins U1, p. 8
melón (m.): melon U12, p. 31
mensajero (m.): messenger, courier U22, p. 50
merendar: to have an afternoon snack U13, p. 32
mermelada (f.): jam U13, p. 33

mes (m.): month U18, p. 42
mesa (f.): table U8, p. 23
mesero (m.): waiter U13, p. 32
mesita de noche (f.): nightstand U8, p. 23
meter un gol: to score a goal U16, p. 39
mexicano: Mexican U24, p. 56
México: Mexico U24, p. 56
microondas (m.): microwave U8, p. 23
miércoles (m.): Wednesday U18, p. 43
mil: a thousand U19, p. 45
(un) millón (m.): a million U19, p. 45
minuto (m.): minute U18, p. 43
mirar un mapa: to look at a map U21, p. 49
mochila (f.): backpack U21, p. 49
moneda (f.): coin U22, p. 50
mono (m.): monkey U23, p. 53
montaña (f.): mountain U17, p. 40
montar a caballo: to ride horses, to go horseback riding
    U17, p. 41
    ~ en bicicleta: to ride a bike U16, p. 38
mora (f.): blackberry U12, p. 31
mosquito (m.): mosquito U23, p. 53
mostrador (m.): counter U21, p. 49
moto (f.): motorcycle U9, p. 25
motor (m.): engine U20, p. 47
mudarse: to move U7, p. 21
muela (f.): molar U6, p. 19
mugir: to moo U23, p. 52
mujer (f.): woman U2, p. 10
multa (f.): ticket U20, p. 47
muñeca (f.): wrist U6, p. 19
muñeco (m.): doll U15, p. 36
    ~ de nieve (m.): snowman U17, p. 41
museo (m.): museum U15, p. 37
músico (m.): musician U15, p. 37

n

nadar: to swim U16, p. 39
    ~ estilo crol: to swim the crawl U16, p. 39
    ~ estilo espalda: to swim (the) backstroke U16, p. 39
    ~ estilo mariposa: to swim butterfly U16, p. 39
    ~ estilo pecho: to swim (the) breaststroke U16, p. 39
nalgas (f.): bottom, buttocks U6, p. 19
naranja (f.): orange U12, p. 31
nariz (f.): nose U6, p. 19
natación (f.): swimming U16, p. 38
navegar (por Internet, la red): to surf (the Internet, the
    Web) U14, p. 35
Navidad (f.): Christmas U18, p. 42
negro (ser ~): black (to be ~) U19, p. 45
nervioso (estar ~): nervous (to be ~) U3, p. 12
nevar: to snow U17, p. 40
nevera (f.): refrigerator U8, p. 23
Nicaragua: Nicaragua U24, p. 56
nicaragüense: Nicaraguan U24, p. 56
nieta (f.): granddaughter U1, p. 9
nieto (m.): grandson U1, p. 9
niño (m.): child, boy U2, p. 10
(en la/por la) noche: at night U18, p. 43
nombre (m.): first name U22, p. 51
Norte: North U24, p. 56
Noruega: Norway U24, p. 56
noruego: Norwegian U24, p. 56
noveno: ninth U19, p. 45
noventa: ninety U19, p. 45

novia (f.): girlfriend U1, p. 8
noviembre: November U18, p. 42
novio (m.): boyfriend U1, p. 8
nube (f.): cloud U17, p. 40
nublado (estar ~): cloudy (to be ~), overcast
    (to be ~) U17, p. 40
nuera (f.): daughter-in-law U1, p. 8
nueve: nine U19, p. 44
nuevo (estar/ser ~): new (to be ~) U19, p. 44
nuez (f.): walnut U12, p. 31

o

obediente (ser ~): obedient (to be ~) U3, p. 12
obra de teatro (f.): play U15, p. 37
Occidente: West U24, p. 56
Oceanía: Oceania U24, p. 56
Océano Atlántico: Atlantic Ocean U24, p. 56
    ~ Índico: Indian Ocean U24, p. 56
    ~ Pacífico: Pacific Ocean U24, p. 56
ochenta: eighty U19, p. 45
ocho: eight U19, p. 44
octavo: eighth U19, p. 45
octubre: October U18, p. 42
odiar: to hate U3, p. 13
Oeste: West U24, p. 56
(de) oferta (estar ~): on sale (to be ~) U10, p. 27
ofertas (f.): sales U10, p. 26
oficina de cambio (f.): exchange bureau U21, p. 49
    ~ de correos (f.): post office U22, p. 50
    ~ de turismo (f.): tourist bureau U21, p. 49
oído (m.): ear U6, p. 19
ojo (m.): eye U6, p. 19
ola (f.): wave U17, p. 41
once: eleven U19, p. 44
óptica (f.): optician U10, p. 27
optimista (ser ~): optimistic (to be ~) U3, p. 12
ordenado (ser ~): neat (to be ~) U3, p. 13
oreja (f.): ear U6, p. 19
orgulloso (estar ~): proud (to be ~) U3, p. 13
Oriente: East U24, p. 56
orilla (f.): shore U17, p. 41
orquesta (f.): orchestra U15, p. 37
oso (m.): bear U23, p. 53
otoño (m.): fall U17, p. 40
oveja (f.): sheep U23, p. 52

p

paciente (m.): patient U6, p. 18
padre (m.): father U1, p. 9
padres (m.): parents U1, p. 9
pagar con tarjeta: to pay with a credit card U11, p. 28
    ~ en efectivo: to pay (in) cash U11, p. 28
país (m.): country U21, p. 48
Países Bajos (Holanda): The Netherlands
    (Holland) U24, p. 56
pájaro (m.): bird U23, p. 52
pajita (f.): straw U13, p. 33
palacio municipal (m.): city hall U9, p. 24
palo de golf (m.): golf club U16, p. 38
pan (m.): bread U13, p. 33
panadería (f.): bakery U11, p. 29
panadero (m.): baker U11, p. 29
Panamá: Panama U24, p. 56

panameño: Panamanian U24, p. 56
pañoleta (f.): scarf U4, p. 15
pantalla (f.): screen U14, p. 35
pantalón (m.): pants U4, p. 15
  ~ corto (m.): shorts U16, p. 38
pantalones (m.): pants U4, p. 15
  ~ vaqueros (m.): jeans U4, p. 15
pantuflas (f.): slippers U4, p. 15
pañuelo (m.): scarf U4, p. 15
papa (f.): potato U12, p. 30
papá (m.): father U1, p. 9
papalote (m.): kite U15, p. 37
papel higiénico (m.): toilet paper U8, p. 23
papelería (f.): stationery store U10, p. 27
paquete (m.): package U11, p. 29, U22, p. 50
parabrisas (m.): windshield U20, p. 47
parachoques (m.): bumper U20, p. 47
parada de autobús (f.): bus stop U9, p. 25
  ~ de taxis (f.): taxi stand U9, p. 25
paraguas (m.): umbrella U4, p. 14
Paraguay: Paraguay U24, p. 56
paraguayo: Paraguayan U24, p. 56
parecerse a alguien: to look like someone U2, p. 10
pared (f.): wall U7, p. 21
párpado (m.): eyelid U6, p. 19
parque (m.): park U9, p. 24
pasado mañana: the day after tomorrow U18, p. 43
pasajero (m.): passenger U21, p. 48
pasaporte (m.): passport U21, p. 48
pasar: to pass U20, p. 46
  ~ la pelota: to pass (the ball) U16, p. 39
pasear: to go for a walk U15, p. 36
pasillo (m.): hallway U7, p. 21
pasta (f.): pasta U11, p. 29
  ~ de dientes: toothpaste U8, p. 23
pastel de cumpleaños (m.): birthday cake U1, p. 8
pastelería (f.): bakery U10, p. 27
pasto (f.): grass U17, p. 41
pata (f.): leg U23, p. 53
patinar: to roller-skate U15, p. 36
patineta (f.): skateboard U15, p. 36
patrulla (f.): patrol car U22, p. 51
peaje (m.): toll U20, p. 46
peatón (m.): pedestrian U9, p. 25
pecho (m.): chest U6, p. 19
pedir: to ask for U11, p. 28; to order U13, p. 32
pegamento (m.): glue U14, p. 35
peinarse: to comb one's hair U1, p. 9
peine (m.): comb U8, p. 23
peinilla (f.): comb U8, p. 23
película (f.): film U15, p. 37
pelirrojo (ser ~): red-haired (to be ~), red hair
  (to have) U2, p. 11
pelota (f.): ball U16, p. 39
peluquería (f.): hair salon U10, p. 27
peluquero (m.): hairdresser U10, p. 27
penthouse (m.): penthouse U7, p. 20
pepino (m.): cucumber U12, p. 30
pequeño (estar/ser ~): small (to be ~), little
  (to be ~) U19, p. 44
pera (f.): pear U12, p. 31
percha (f.): hanger U4, p. 14
perchero (m.): coat rack U8, p. 22
perder: to lose U16, p. 38
  ~ el avión: to miss the plane U21, p. 48
perejil (m.): parsley U12, p. 30

perfumería (f.): drug store U10, p. 27
periodista (m.): journalist U5, p. 16
perro (m.): dog U23, p. 52
persiana (f.): blind U7, p. 21
persona con discapacidad auditiva: deaf, hearing
  impaired U2, p. 10
  ~ con discapacidad física: physically
    challenged U2, p. 10
  ~ con discapacidad visual: blind, sight
    impaired U2, p. 10
Perú: Peru U24, p. 56
peruano: Peruvian U24, p. 56
pesar: to weigh U11, p. 28
pesas (f.): weights U16, p. 39
pescadería (f.): fish market U11, p. 29
pescadero (m.): fishmonger U11, p. 29
pescado (m.): fish U11, p. 29
pescar: to fish, to go fishing U17, p. 41
pesimista (ser ~): pessimistic (to be ~) U3, p. 12
pestañas (f.): eyelashes U6, p. 19
pez (m.): fish U23, p. 53
piano (m.): piano U15, p. 37
piar: to chirp, to tweet U23, p. 52
picar: to sting, to bite U23, p. 52
pie (m.): foot U6, p. 19
(de) pie (estar ~): standing (to be ~) U6, p. 19
pierna (f.): leg U6, p. 19
pijama (m./f.): pajamas U4, p. 15
piloto (m.): pilot U21, p. 48
pimienta (f.): pepper U13, p. 33
pimiento (m.): bell pepper U12, p. 30
piña (f.): pineapple U12, p. 31
pinchar una llanta: to get a flat tire U20, p. 47
pingüino (m.): penguin U23, p. 53
piñón (m.): pine nut U12, p. 31
pintar: to paint U15, p. 36
pintor (m.): painter U5, p. 17
piscina (f.): swimming pool U16, p. 39
piso (m.): floor U7, p. 21
pista de aterrizaje (f.): runway U21, p. 48
pistache (m.): pistachio U12, p. 31
pistacho (m.): pistachio U12, p. 31
piyama (m./f.): pajamas U4, p. 15
placa (f.): license plate U20, p. 47
plancha (f.): iron U8, p. 23
planta (f.): plant U10, p. 27
  ~ baja (f.): first floor, ground floor U7, p. 20
plátano (m.): banana U12, p. 31
plato fuerte (m.): second course U13, p. 33
  ~ hondo (m.): soup dish U13, p. 33
  ~ llano (m.): (dinner) plate U13, p. 33
playa (f.): beach U17, p. 40
plaza (f.): square U9, p. 24
plomero (m.): plumber U5, p. 17
podrido (estar ~): rotten (to be ~) U12, p. 31
polaco: Polish U24, p. 56
policía (f.): police officer U22, p. 51
pollo (m.): chicken U11, p. 29
Polonia: Poland U24, p. 56
ponerse: to put on U4, p. 14
  ~ bloqueador solar: to put on sunscreen U17, p. 41
portafolios (m.): briefcase U14, p. 35
portería (f.): goal U16, p. 39
portero (m.): goalkeeper U16, p. 39; doorman U7, p. 21
portugués: Portuguese U24, p. 56
postal (f.): postcard U22, p. 50

postre (m.): dessert U13, p. 33
precio (m.): price U10, p. 26
preguntar: to ask U9, p. 25
prender: to turn on U14, p. 35
preocupado (estar ~): worried (to be ~) U3, p. 12
prima (f.): cousin U1, p. 9
primavera (f.): spring U17, p. 40
primer piso (m.): second floor U7, p. 20
   ~ plato (m.): first course U13, p. 33
primero: first U19, p. 45
primo (m.): cousin U1, p. 9
probador (m.): fitting room U4, p. 14
probarse: to try on U4, p. 14
profesor (m.): teacher, professor U5, p. 17
psicólogo (m.): psychologist U5, p. 17
pueblo (m.): town, village U17, p. 41
puente (m.): overpass U20, p. 46
puerro (m.): leek U12, p. 30
puerta (f.): door U7, p. 21
   ~ de embarque (f.): gate U21, p. 48
puesto de periódicos (m.): kiosk U10, p. 27
pulpo (m.): octopus U23, p. 53
pulsera (f.): bracelet U4, p. 15
pupila (f.): pupil U6, p. 19

q

quedar: to arrange to meet, to meet (up with) U15, p. 36
querer: to love U3, p. 13
queso (m.): cheese U11, p. 29
quince: fifteen U19, p. 44
quinto: fifth U19, p. 45
quiosco (m.): newspaper kiosk U10, p. 27
quitarse: to take off U4, p. 14

r

rábano (m.): radish U12, p. 30
radiador (m.): radiator U20, p. 47
radiografía (f.): X-ray U6, p. 18
ramo de rosas (m.): bouquet of roses U10, p. 27
rana (f.): frog U23, p. 52
raqueta (f.): racket U16, p. 39
rascacielos (m.): skyscraper U9, p. 24
ratón (m.): mouse U14, p. 35
(a) rayas (ser ~): striped (to be ~) U4, p. 14
rebajas (f.): sales U10, p. 26
recepción (f.): reception desk U14, p. 34; reception U21, p. 49
recepcionista (f.): receptionist U21, p. 49
receta (f.): prescription U6, p. 18
recibidor (m.): entrance hall U8, p. 22
recibir una carta: to receive a letter U22, p. 50
recibo (m.): receipt U10, p. 26
recoger el equipaje: to pick up the luggage U21, p. 48
red (f.): net U16, p. 39
redondo (ser ~): round (to be ~) U19, p. 44
refrigerador (m.): refrigerator U8, p. 23
regalo (m.): gift U1, p. 8
Reino Unido: United Kingdom U24, p. 56
reír: to laugh U3, p. 13
relinchar: to neigh, to whinny U23, p. 52
reloj (m.): watch U4, p. 15
   ~ de pared (m.): clock U8, p. 23
remitente (m.): sender U22, p. 51

remolacha (f.): beet U12, p. 30
repartir el correo: to deliver the mail, to post U22, p. 50
repollo (m.): cabbage U12, p. 30
República Dominicana: Dominican Republic U24, p. 56
reunión (f.): meeting U14, p. 34
reunirse: to meet U14, p. 34
revisar el equipaje: to check luggage U21, p. 48
rico (estar ~): good (to be ~), delicious (to be ~) U13, p. 32
rin (m.): hubcap U20, p. 47
río (m.): river U17, p. 41
robar: to steal (something), to rob (a person or place) U22, p. 50
rodilla (f.): knee U6, p. 19
rojo (ser ~): red (to be ~) U19, p. 45
rubio (ser ~): blond (to be ~) U2, p. 11
rueda (f.): tire, wheel U20, p. 47
rugir: to roar U23, p. 52
Rusia: Russia U24, p. 56
ruso: Russian U24, p. 56

s

sábado (m.): Saturday U18, p. 43
sábanas (f.): sheets U8, p. 23
sacar dinero: to withdraw money, to take out money U22, p. 51
sacerdote (m.): priest U5, p. 16
saco (m.): jacket U4, p. 15
   ~ de dormir (m.): sleeping bag U17, p. 41
sal (f.): salt U13, p. 33
sala (f.): living room U8, p. 22
   ~ de espera (f.): waiting room U6, p. 18
   ~ de urgencias (f.): emergency room U6, p. 18
salida (f.): exit U10, p. 27; exit U20, p. 46
   ~ de emergencia (f.): emergency exit U10, p. 26
salidas (f.): departures U21, p. 48
salir: to go out, to leave U9, p. 24
salón (m.): living room U8, p. 22
saltar: to jump U16, p. 39
   ~ a la cuerda: to skip U15, p. 37
salvadoreño: Salvadorian U24, p. 56
salvaje (ser ~): wild (to be ~) U23, p. 52
salvavidas (m.): lifeguard U17, p. 41
sandalias (f.): sandals U4, p. 15
sandía (f.): watermelon U12, p. 31
sándwich (m.): sandwich U13, p. 33
secador (m.): hair dryer U8, p. 23
secretario (m.): secretary U14, p. 34
seguir derecho: to go straight U9, p. 24
   ~ recto: to go straight U9, p. 24
segundo: second U18, p. 43, U19, p. 45
   ~ piso (m.): third floor U7, p. 20
   ~ plato (m.): second course U13, p. 33
seis: six U19, p. 44
sello (m.): stamp U22, p. 51
semáforo (m.): traffic light U9, p. 25
semana (f.): week U18, p. 42
señal de tráfico (f.): traffic sign U20, p. 46
sentado (estar ~): sitting (to be ~), seated (to be ~) U6, p. 19
septiembre: September U18, p. 42
séptimo: seventh U19, p. 45
serio (ser ~): serious (to be ~) U3, p. 12
serpiente (f.): snake U23, p. 53
servicio de habitaciones (m.): room service U21, p. 49

servilleta (f.): napkin U13, p. 32
sesenta: sixty U19, p. 45
setenta: seventy U19, p. 45
sexto: sixth U19, p. 45
siete: seven U19, p. 44
silla (f.): chair U8, p. 23
sillón (m.): armchair U8, p. 23
simpático (ser ~): friendly (to be ~) U3, p. 12
sobre (m.): envelope U22, p. 51
sobrina (f.): niece U1, p. 8
sobrino (m.): nephew U1, p. 8
sociable (ser ~): sociable (to be ~) U3, p. 12
sofá (m.): sofa, couch U8, p. 23
sol (m.): sun U17, p. 40
soldado (m.): soldier U5, p. 16
soltero (estar/ser ~): single (to be ~) U1, p. 8
sombrero (m.): hat U4, p. 15
sombrilla (f.): beach umbrella U17, p. 41
son las cinco y cuarto: it's quarter after five U18, p. 43
  ~ las cuatro y cinco: it's five after four U18, p. 43
  ~ las diez de la noche: it's ten o'clock at night, it's ten p.m. U18, p. 43
  ~ las nueve de la mañana: it's nine o'clock in the morning, it's nine a.m. U18, p. 43
  ~ las ocho menos diez: it's ten of eight U18, p. 43
  ~ las seis y media: it's six thirty U18, p. 43
  ~ las siete menos cuarto: it's quarter of seven, it's quarter till seven U18, p. 43
sopa (f.): soup U13, p. 33
sopera (f.): soup tureen U13, p. 33
sordo (estar ~): deaf (to be ~), hearing impaired U2, p. 10
sorprendido (estar ~): surprised (to be ~) U3, p. 13
sortija (f.): ring U4, p. 15
sostén (m.): bra U4, p. 15
subibaja (m.): seesaw U15, p. 37
subir al autobús: to get on a bus U9, p. 25
sucio (estar ~): dirty (to be ~) U8, p. 22
sudadera (m.): sweatsuit U16, p. 38
Suecia: Sweden U24, p. 56
sueco: Swedish U24, p. 56
suegra (f.): mother-in-law U1, p. 8
suéter (m.): sweater U4, p. 15
Suiza: Switzerland U24, p. 56
suizo: Swiss U24, p. 56
sujetapapeles (m.): paper clip U14, p. 35
sujetador (m.): bra U4, p. 15
Sur: South U24, p. 56
Suráfrica: South Africa U24, p. 56
surafricano: South African U24, p. 56

t

tablero de anuncios (m.): notice board U14, p. 34
tableta de chocolate (f.): chocolate bar U11, p. 29
talla (f.): size U4, p. 14
taller (m.): workshop U5, p. 17
taquilla (f.): box office U15, p. 37
(en la/por la) tarde: in the afternoon, in the evening U18, p. 43
tarjeta de crédito (f.): credit card U22, p. 50
  ~ de débito (f.): debit card U22, p. 50
  ~ de embarque (f.): boarding pass U21, p. 49
  ~ de presentación (f.): business card U14, p. 35
tarta de manzana (f.): apple pie U13, p. 33
taxi (m.): taxi U9, p. 25
taxista (m.): taxi driver U9, p. 25

taza (f.): cup U13, p. 33
té (m.): tea U13, p. 33
teatro (m.): theater U15, p. 37
techo (m.): ceiling, roof U7, p. 21
teclado (m.): keyboard U14, p. 35
técnico en informática (m.): computer technician U5, p. 17
tejado (m.): roof U7, p. 21
tejer: to knit U15, p. 36
teléfono (m.): telephone U14, p. 35
telegrama (m.): telegram U22, p. 50
televisor (m.): television U8, p. 23
tender la cama: to make the bed U8, p. 22
tenedor (m.): fork U13, p. 33
tener barba: to have a beard U2, p. 11
  ~ bigote: to have a mustache U2, p. 11
  ~ buena figura: to have a good figure U2, p. 10
  ~ calor: to be hot U3, p. 13
  ~ canas: to have gray hair U2, p. 11
  ~ colitas: to have a ponytail U2, p. 11
  ~ el pelo canoso: to have white hair U2, p. 11
  ~ el pelo corto: to have short hair U2, p. 11
  ~ el pelo largo: to have long hair U2, p. 11
  ~ el pelo liso: to have straight hair U2, p. 11
  ~ el pelo rizado: to have curly hair U2, p. 11
  ~ fiebre: to have a fever U6, p. 18
  ~ frío: to be cold U3, p. 13
  ~ gripa: to have the flu U6, p. 18
  ~ gripe: to have the flu U6, p. 18
  ~ hambre: to be hungry U3, p. 13
  ~ los ojos azules: to have blue eyes U2, p. 11
  ~ los ojos de color café: to have brown eyes U2, p. 11
  ~ los ojos grandes: to have big eyes U2, p. 11
  ~ los ojos marrones: to have brown eyes U2, p. 11
  ~ los ojos negros: to have black eyes U2, p. 11
  ~ los ojos pequeños: to have small eyes U2, p. 11
  ~ los ojos verdes: to have green eyes U2, p. 11
  ~ miedo: to be afraid U3, p. 13
  ~ ojos claros: to have light-colored eyes U2, p. 11
  ~ ojos oscuros: to have dark eyes U2, p. 11
  ~ pecas: to have freckles U2, p. 11
  ~ pelo castaño: to be brown-haired, to have brown hair U2, p. 11
  ~ pelo negro: to be dark-haired U2, p. 11
  ~ pelo rubio: to be blond U2, p. 11
  ~ puesta una gorra: to wear a cap U2, p. 11
  ~ sed: to be thirsty U3, p. 13
  ~ sueño: to be sleepy, to be tired U3, p. 13
  ~ trenzas: to have braids U2, p. 11
  ~ un lunar: to have a mole, to have a beauty mark U2, p. 11
  ~ un resfriado: to have a cold, to be congested U6, p. 18
  ~ una cita: to have an appointment U14, p. 35
  ~ una empresa: to have a business U5, p. 17
tenis (m.): tennis U16, p. 38
tercer piso (m.): fourth floor U7, p. 20
tercero: third U19, p. 45
termómetro (m.): thermometer U6, p. 18
terraza (f.): terrace U7, p. 21
tetera (f.): teapot U13, p. 33
tía (f.): aunt U1, p. 8
tiburón (m.): shark U23, p. 53
ticket (m.): receipt U10, p. 26

tienda de discos (f.): record store U10, p. 27
  ~ de electrodomésticos (f.): appliance store U10, p. 27
  ~ de ropa (f.): clothing store U10, p. 27
tigre (m.): tiger U23, p. 53
timbre (m.): doorbell U7, p. 21; stamp U22, p. 51
tímido (ser ~): shy (to be ~) U3, p. 12
tina (f.): bathtub U8, p. 23
tintorería (f.): drycleaners U10, p. 27
tío (m.): uncle U1, p. 8
tirar al bote de basura: to throw in the trash can U9, p. 25
tirarse de cabeza: to dive U16, p. 39
toalla (f.): towel U8, p. 23
tobillo (m.): ankle U6, p. 19
tobogán (m.): slide U15, p. 37
tocar un instrumento: to play an instrument U15, p. 37
tomar algo: to have a drink U15, p. 36
  ~ el sol: to sunbathe U17, p. 41
  ~ el tren: to take the train U9, p. 25
  ~ fotografías: to take photos U15, p. 36
tomate (m.): tomato U12, p. 30
tortuga (f.): turtle U23, p. 53
toser: to cough U6, p. 18
trabajador (ser ~): hardworking (to be ~) U3, p. 12
trabajar: to work U14, p. 34
  ~ en una fábrica: to work in a factory U5, p. 17
tractor (m.): tractor U17, p. 41
traer el menú: to bring the menu U13, p. 32
  ~ la carta: to bring the menu U13, p. 32
  ~ la cuenta: to bring the check U13, p. 32
traje (m.): suit U4, p. 15
  ~ de baño (m.): swimsuit U4, p. 15
trampolín (m.): diving board U16, p. 39
tranquilo (estar ~): calm (to be ~) U3, p. 12
trasero (m.): bottom, buttocks U6, p. 19
travieso (ser ~): mischievous (to be ~) U3, p. 12
trece: thirteen U19, p. 44
treinta: thirty U19, p. 45
tren (m.): train U9, p. 25
tres: three U19, p. 44
triciclo (m.): tricycle U15, p. 36
triste (estar ~): sad (to be ~) U3, p. 12
trituradora de papel (f.): shredder U14, p. 35
trompeta (f.): trumpet U15, p. 37
túnel (m.): tunnel U20, p. 46
turco: Turkish U24, p. 56
turista (m./f.): tourist U21, p. 49
Turquía: Turkey U24, p. 56

u

universidad (f.): university U5, p. 17
uno: one U19, p. 44
urdu: Urdu U24, p. 56
Uruguay: Uruguay U24, p. 56
uruguayo: Uruguayan U24, p. 56
usar gafas: to wear glasses U2, p. 11
  ~ lentes: to wear glasses U2, p. 11
uva (f.): grape U12, p. 31

v

vaca (f.): cow U23, p. 52
vacío (estar ~): empty (to be ~) U10, p. 27
vago (ser ~): lazy (to be ~) U3, p. 12
valle (m.): valley U17, p. 41
vaqueros (m.): jeans U4, p. 15
vaso (m.): glass U13, p. 33
vecino (m.): neighbor U7, p. 21
veinte: twenty U19, p. 45
vela (f.): candle U1, p. 8
vendedor (m.): sales representative U5, p. 16; clerk U10, p. 27
vender: to sell U7, p. 21
venenoso (ser ~): poisonous (to be ~) U23, p. 52
venezolano: Venezuelan U24, p. 56
Venezuela: Venezuela U24, p. 56
ventana (f.): window U7, p. 21
ventanilla (f.): window U21, p. 49, U22, p. 51
ver la televisión: to watch TV U1, p. 9
verano (m.): summer U17, p. 40
verde (estar): unripe (to be ~), green (to be ~) U12, p. 31
  ~ (ser ~): green (to be ~) U19, p. 45
verdura (f.): vegetables U11, p. 29
vestido (m.): dress U4, p. 15
vestirse: to get dressed U1, p. 9
veterinario (m.): veterinarian, vet U5, p. 17
viejito (m.): elderly person, old man U2, p. 10
viejo (estar/ser ~): old (to be ~), older (to be ~) U19, p. 44
viernes (m.): Friday U18, p. 43
vietnamita: Vietnamese U24, p. 56
vinagre (m.): vinegar U13, p. 33
violín (m.): violin U15, p. 37
visitar una exposición: to see an exhibition U15, p. 37
vitrina (f.): glass cabinet U8, p. 23
viudo (estar/ser ~): widowed (to be ~) U1, p. 8
volante (m.): steering wheel U20, p. 47
volar: to fly U21, p. 48
vomitar: to throw up, to vomit U6, p. 18
vuelo (m.): flight U21, p. 49

y

yerno (m.): son-in-law U1, p. 8
yogur (m.): yogurt U11, p. 29

z

zanahoria (f.): carrot U12, p. 30
zapatería (f.): shoe store U10, p. 27
zapatillas de tenis (f.): sneakers, tennis shoes U16, p. 38
zapatos (m.): shoes U4, p. 15
  ~ de tacón (m.): high-heeled shoes U4, p. 15
zumo (m.): juice U11, p. 29

English-Spanish Glossary

a

above (to be ~): arriba (estar ~) U7, p. 20
absentminded (to be ~): despistado (ser ~) U3, p. 13
accelerate: acelerar U20, p. 46
accident: choque U20, p. 47
actor: actor U5, p. 16
actress: actriz U5, p. 16
address: dirección U22, p. 51
addressee: destinatario U22, p. 51
adolescent: adolescente U2, p. 10
adult: adulto U2, p. 10
affectionate (to be ~): cariñoso (ser ~) U3, p. 13
afraid (to be ~): tener miedo U3, p. 13
Africa: África U24, p. 56
(in the) afternoon: en la tarde, por la tarde U18, p. 43
air conditioning: aire acondicionado U7, p. 21
airline: compañía aérea U21, p. 49
airplane: avión U21, p. 49
airport: aeropuerto U21, p. 48
alarm: alarma U22, p. 51
  ~clock: despertador U8, p. 23
almond: almendra U12, p. 31
ambulance: ambulancia U6, p. 18
American: estadounidense U24, p. 56
angry (to be ~): enojado (estar ~) U3, p. 13
ankle: tobillo U6, p. 19
answer: contestar U9, p. 25
Antarctica: Antártida U24, p. 56
antenna: antena U7, p. 21
apartment: apartamento U7, p. 20
  ~building: edificio de apartamentos U9, p. 24
applaud: aplaudir U15, p. 36
apple: manzana U12, p. 31
  ~pie: tarta de manzana U13, p. 33
appliance store: tienda de electrodomésticos U10, p. 27
April: abril U18, p. 42
Arabic: árabe U24, p. 56
architect: arquitecto U5, p. 17
architect's studio: estudio de arquitectura U5, p. 17
Argentina: Argentina U24, p. 56
Argentinian: argentino U24, p. 56
arm: brazo U6, p. 19
armchair: sillón U8, p. 23
arrange to meet: quedar U15, p. 36
arrest: detener U22, p. 51
arrivals: llegadas U21, p. 48
arrive late: llegar tarde U14, p. 34
artichoke: alcachofa U12, p. 30
Asia: Asia U24, p. 56
ask: preguntar U9, p. 25
  ~for: pedir U11, p. 28
asparagus: espárrago U12, p. 30
"at" symbol: arroba U14, p. 35
Atlantic Ocean: Océano Atlántico U24, p. 56
August: agosto U18, p. 42
aunt: tía U1, p. 8
Australia: Australia U24, p. 56
Australian: australiano U24, p. 56
Austria: Austria U24, p. 56
Austrian: austriaco U24, p. 56
automated teller machine (ATM): cajero automático U22, p. 50
avenue: avenida U9, p. 24

avocado: aguacate U12, p. 31

b

baby: bebé U2, p. 10
back: espalda U6, p. 19; animal lomo U23, p. 53
backpack: mochila U21, p. 49
bag: bolsa U10, p. 26
baggage: equipaje U21, p. 49
baker: panadero U11, p. 29
bakery: pastelería U10, p. 27; panadería U11, p. 29
bald (to be ~): calvo (estar ~) U2, p. 11
ball: pelota U16, p. 39
banana: plátano U12, p. 31
bank: banco U22, p. 50
bark: ladrar U23, p. 52
baseball: béisbol U16, p. 38
  ~glove: guante de béisbol U16, p. 39
basket: canasta U16, p. 39
basketball: basquetbol, básquetbol U16, p. 38
bat: bate U16, p. 39
bathroom: (cuarto de) baño U8, p. 22
bathtub: bañera, tina U8, p. 23
battery: batería U20, p. 47
beach: playa U17, p. 40
  ~umbrella: sombrilla U17, p. 41
bean: frijol U12, p. 31
bear: oso U23, p. 53
bed: cama U8, p. 23
bedroom: habitación U8, p. 22
bee: abeja U23, p. 53
beef: carne de res U11, p. 29
beet: remolacha U12, p. 30
behind (to be ~): atrás (estar ~), detrás (estar ~) U7, p. 20
Belgian: belga U24, p. 56
Belgium: Bélgica U24, p. 56
bell pepper: pimiento U12, p. 30
below (to be ~): abajo (estar ~) U7, p. 20
belt: cinturón U4, p. 14
bench: banco U9, p. 25
Bengali: bengalí U24, p. 56
between (to be ~): entre (estar ~) U7, p. 20
bicycle: bicicleta U16, p. 38
big (to be ~): grande (estar/ser ~) U19, p. 44
bikini: bikini U4, p. 15
bill: billete U22, p. 50
bird: pájaro U23, p. 52
birthday cake: pastel de cumpleaños U1, p. 8
  ~party: fiesta de cumpleaños U1, p. 8
bite: picar U23, p. 52
black (to be ~): negro (ser ~) U19, p. 45
blackberry: mora U12, p. 31
bleat: balar U23, p. 52
blind: ciego (estar ~), persona con discapacidad visual U2, p. 10; persiana U7, p. 21
block: cuadra, manzana U9, p. 24
blond (to be ~): tener pelo rubio, rubio (ser ~) U2, p. 11
blouse: blusa U4, p. 15
blue (to be ~): azul (ser ~) U19, p. 45
blueberry: arándano U12, p. 31
board: embarcar U21, p. 48
boarding pass: tarjeta de embarque U21, p. 49
Bolivia: Bolivia U24, p. 56
Bolivian: boliviano U24, p. 56
bookshelf: estantería, librero U8, p. 23

bookstore: librería U10, p. 27
boots: botas U4, p. 15
bored (to be ~): aburrido (estar ~) U3, p. 13
boss: jefe U14, p. 34
bottle: botella U11, p. 29
bottom: nalgas, trasero U6, p. 19
bouquet of roses: ramo de rosas U10, p. 27
bowl: bol U13, p. 33
box: caja U11, p. 29
   ~office: boletería, taquilla U15, p. 37
boy: niño U2, p. 10
boyfriend: novio U1, p. 8
bra: sostén, sujetador U4, p. 15
bracelet: pulsera U4, p. 15
brake: frenar U20, p. 46
Brazil: Brasil U24, p. 56
Brazilian: brasileño U24, p. 56
bread: pan U13, p. 33
break down: averiarse, descomponerse U20, p. 47
bricklayer: albañil U5, p. 17
briefcase: portafolios, maletín U14, p. 35
bring the check: traer la cuenta U13, p. 32
   ~the menu: traer la carta, traer el menú U13, p. 32
British: británico U24, p. 56
broccoli: brócoli U12, p. 30
brother: hermano U1, p. 9
brother-in-law: cuñado U1, p. 8
brown (to be ~): café (ser ~) U19, p. 45
brown-haired (to be ~): tener pelo castaño U2, p. 11
brush one's teeth: lavarse los dientes U1, p. 9
building: edificio U7, p. 20
   ~apartment building edificio de apartamentos U9, p. 24
bumper: defensas, parachoques U20, p. 47
bus: autobús U9, p. 25
   ~driver: chofer U5, p. 16
   ~stop: parada de autobús U9, p. 25
business card: tarjeta de presentación U14, p. 35
   ~man: empresario U5, p. 17
butcher: carnicero U11, p. 29
   ~shop: carnicería U11, p. 29
butter: mantequilla U13, p. 33
butterfly: mariposa U23, p. 53
buttocks: nalgas, trasero U6, p. 19
button (up): abrocharse U4, p. 14
buy: comprar U10, p. 26

C

cabbage: col, repollo U12, p. 30
café: cafetería U15, p. 36
calculator: calculadora U14, p. 35
calendar: agenda U14, p. 35; calendario U18, p. 42
calm (to be ~): tranquilo (estar ~) U3, p. 12
camera: cámara fotográfica, cámara de fotos U15, p. 36
camp: acampar U17, p. 41
can: lata U11, p. 29
Canada: Canadá U24, p. 56
Canadian: canadiense U24, p. 56
candle: vela U1, p. 8
canned goods: conservas U11, p. 28
canteen: cantimplora U17, p. 41
cap: gorra U16, p. 39
capital (city): capital U21, p. 48
car: auto U9, p. 25
carnivorous (to be ~): carnívoro (ser ~) U23, p. 52
carousel: carrusel U15, p. 37

carpenter: carpintero U5, p. 17
carrot: zanahoria U12, p. 30
cart: carrito U21, p. 49
carton: envase de cartón U11, p. 29
cashier: cajero U11, p. 28
(in a) cast (to be ~): enyesado (estar ~) U6, p. 18
cat: gato U23, p. 52
cauliflower: coliflor U12, p. 30
ceiling: techo U7, p. 21
celery: apio U12, p. 30
cell phone: celular (teléfono) U14, p. 35
(in the) center (to be ~): (en el) centro (estar ~) U7, p. 20
cereal: cereales U13, p. 33
certified mail: correo certificado U22, p. 50
chair: silla U8, p. 23
cheap (to be ~): barato (ser ~) U11, p. 28
check: cheque U22, p. 51
   ~a map: consultar un mapa U21, p. 49
   ~in luggage: facturar el equipaje U21, p. 49
   ~luggage: revisar el equipaje U21, p. 48
checkout: caja U11, p. 28
cheek: cachete, mejilla U6, p. 19
cheese: queso U11, p. 29
chef: cocinero U13, p. 32
cherry: cereza U12, p. 31
chest: pecho U6, p. 19
chicken: pollo U11, p. 29
chickpea: garbanzo U12, p. 31
child: niño U2, p. 10
Chile: Chile U24, p. 56
Chilean: chileno U24, p. 56
chimney: chimenea U7, p. 21
China: China U24, p. 56
Chinese: chino U24, p. 56
chirp: piar U23, p. 52
chocolate bar: barra de chocolate, tableta de chocolate U11, p. 29
Christmas: Navidad U18, p. 42
church: iglesia U9, p. 24
city hall: palacio municipal U9, p. 24
civil servant: funcionario U5, p. 16
clap: aplaudir U15, p. 36
clean (to be ~): limpio (estar ~) U8, p. 22
   ~the house: limpiar la casa U8, p. 22
cleaning lady: empleada doméstica U5, p. 17
   ~products: artículos de limpieza U11, p. 28
clerk: vendedor U10, p. 26
climb: escalar U17, p. 41
clock: reloj de pared U8, p. 23
closed (to be ~): cerrado (estar ~) U7, p. 21
closet: armario U8, p. 23
clothing store: tienda de ropa U10, p. 27
cloud: nube U17, p. 40
cloudy (to be ~): nublado (estar ~) U17, p. 40
cluck: cacarear U23, p. 52
coach: entrenador U16, p. 39
coat: abrigo U4, p. 15
   ~rack: perchero U8, p. 22
coffee: café U13, p. 33
coffee pot: cafetera U13, p. 33
coffee with milk: café con leche U13, p. 33
coin: moneda U22, p. 50
cold (to be ~): tener frío U3, p. 13; estar frío U13, p. 32; hacer frío U17, p. 40
   ~cuts: embutidos, fiambres U11, p. 29
college graduate (to be ~): licenciado (ser ~) U5, p. 16

Colombia: Colombia U24, p. 56
Colombian: colombiano U24, p. 56
comb: peine, peinilla U8, p. 23
  ~ one's hair: peinarse U1, p. 9
come in: entrar U9, p. 24
comforter: edredón U8, p. 23
company: empresa U14, p. 34
computer technician: técnico en informática U5, p. 17
concert: concierto U15, p. 37
conductor: director U15, p. 37
congested (to be ~): tener un resfriado U6, p. 18
convertible: convertible, descapotable U20, p. 46
cook: cocinar U13, p. 32; cocinero U13, p. 32
cookie: galleta U11, p. 29
corn: maíz U12, p. 30
corner: esquina U9, p. 24
cost: costar U11, p. 28
Costa Rica: Costa Rica U24, p. 56
Costa Rican: costarricense U24, p. 56
couch: sofá U8, p. 23
cough: toser U6, p. 18
counter: mostrador U21, p. 49
country: país U21, p. 48
countryside: campo U17, p. 40
courier: mensajero U22, p. 50
cousin: prima, primo U1, p. 9
cow: vaca U23, p. 52
coworker: compañero U14, p. 34
CPU: CPU U14, p. 35
crash: chocar, choque U20, p. 47
credit card: tarjeta de crédito U22, p. 50
croak: croar U23, p. 52
crocodile: cocodrilo U23, p. 53
cross: cruzar la calle U9, p. 25
crosswalk: cruce peatonal U9, p. 25
crow: cacarear U23, p 52
cry: llorar U3, p. 13
Cuba: Cuba U24, p. 56
Cuban: cubano U24, p. 56
cucumber: pepino U12, p. 30
cup: taza U13, p. 33
curriculum vitae: currículum U14, p. 35
curtains: cortinas U8, p. 23
curve: curva U20, p. 46
customer: cliente U10, p. 26
Customs: aduana U21, p. 48
cut: cortar U11, p. 28
cycling: ciclismo U16, p. 38

delicious (to be ~): delicioso (estar ~), rico
  (estar ~) U13, p. 32
deliver a telegram: entregar un telegrama U22, p. 50
  ~ the mail: repartir el correo U22, p. 50
Denmark: Dinamarca U24, p. 56
dentist: dentista U6, p. 18
departures: salidas U21, p. 48
deposit money: depositar dinero U22, p. 51
desk: escritorio U8, p. 23
  ~ lamp: lámpara U8, p. 23
desktop computer: computadora U14, p. 35
dessert: postre U13, p. 33
destination: destino U21, p. 49
diesel: diésel (fuel) U20, p. 47
diesel (fuel): gasoil U20, p. 47
dining room: comedor U8, p. 22
directory: directorio U10, p. 26
dirty (to be ~): sucio (estar ~) U8, p. 22
disgust: dar asco U3, p. 13
dishwasher: lavaplatos U8, p. 23
dive: clavado, tirarse de cabeza U16, p. 39
diving board: trampolín U16, p. 39
divorced (to be ~): divorciado (estar/ser ~) U1, p. 8
do a load of laundry: lavar en la lavadora U8, p. 22
doctor: médico U6, p. 18
dog: perro U23, p. 52
doll: muneco U15, p. 36
dolphin: delfín U23, p. 53
domestic worker: empleada doméstica U5, p. 17
domesticated: manso (ser ~) U23, p. 52
Dominican: dominicano U24, p. 56
  ~ Republic: República Dominicana U24, p. 56
door: puerta U7, p. 21
doorbell: timbre U7, p. 21
doorman: portero U7, p. 21
double bed: cama matrimonial U8, p. 23
  ~ room: habitación doble U21, p. 49
downtown: centro (de la ciudad) U9, p. 24
dozen eggs: docena de huevos U11, p. 29
dress: vestido U4, p. 15
drink: beber U13, p. 32
drinks: bebidas U11, p. 28
drive: conducir U20, p. 46
driver's license: licencia de conducir U20, p. 47
drug store: perfumería U10, p. 27
drycleaners: tintorería U10, p. 27
Dutch: holandés U24, p. 56
DVD (player): (reproductor de) DVD U8, p. 23

d

dance: bailar U15, p. 36
dancer: bailarín U15, p. 36
Danish: danés U24, p. 56
dark skin (to have ~): bronceado (estar ~) U2, p. 11
dark-haired (to be ~): tener pelo negro U2, p. 11
date: dátil U12, p. 31; fecha U18, p. 42
daughter: hija U1, p. 9
daughter-in-law: nuera U1, p. 8
day: día U18, p. 42
(the) day after tomorrow: pasado mañana U18, p. 43
(the) day before yesterday: antes de ayer U18, p. 43
deaf (to be ~): persona con discapacidad auditiva, sordo
  (estar ~) U2, p. 10
debit card: tarjeta de débito U22, p. 50
December: diciembre U18, p. 42

e

eagle: águila U23, p. 53
ear: oído, oreja U6, p. 19
earrings: aretes U4, p. 15
East: Este, Oriente U24, p. 56
eat: comer U13, p. 32
Ecuador: Ecuador U24, p. 56
Ecuadorian: ecuatoriano U24, p. 56
eggplant: berenjena U12, p. 30
Egypt: Egipto U24, p. 56
Egyptian: egipcio U24, p. 56
eight: ocho U19, p. 44
eighteen: dieciocho U19, p. 45
eighth: octavo U19, p. 45
eighty: ochenta U19, p. 45
El Salvador: El Salvador U24, p. 56

elbow: codo U6, p. 19
elderly person: anciano, viejito U2, p. 10
electric stove: estufa, cocina U8, p. 23
electrician: electricista U5, p. 17
elephant: elefante U23, p. 53
elevator: ascensor, elevador U7, p. 21
eleven: once U19, p. 44
email: escribir un correo electrónico U14, p. 35
embarrassed (to be ~): dar vergüenza U3, p. 13
emergency exit: salida de emergencia U10, p. 26
    ~**room:** sala de urgencias U6, p. 18
employee: empleado U14, p. 34
empty (to be ~): vacío (estar ~) U10, p. 27
engine: motor U20, p. 47
engineer: ingeniero U5, p. 16
English: inglés U24, p. 56
entrance: entrada U10, p. 27
    ~**hall:** recibidor U8, p. 22
envelope: sobre U22, p. 51
envious (to be ~): envidioso (ser ~) U3, p. 13
eraser: goma de borrar U14, p. 35
escalator: escaleras eléctricas, escaleras
    mecánicas U10, p. 26
Europe: Europa U24, p. 56
(in the) evening: en la tarde, por la tarde U18, p. 43
exchange: cambiar U10, p. 26
    ~**bureau:** oficina de cambio U21, p. 49
    ~**money:** cambiar dinero U21, p. 49
executive: ejecutivo U5, p. 17
exercise: hacer ejercicio U16, p. 39
exhibition: exposición U15, p. 37
exit: salida U10, p. 27, U20, p. 46
expensive (to be ~): caro (ser ~) U11, p. 28
eye: ojo U6, p. 19
eyebrows: cejas U6, p. 19
eyelashes: pestañas U6, p. 19
eyelid: párpado U6, p. 19

---

f

factory: fábrica U5, p. 17
fall: otoño U17, p. 40
far (to be ~): lejos (estar ~) U7, p. 20
farmer: agricultor U5, p. 16
fasten: abrocharse U4, p. 14
fat (to be ~): gordo (ser ~) U2, p. 10
father: padre, papá U1, p. 9
faucet: llave, grifo U8, p. 23
fax: fax U14, p. 34
February: febrero U18, p. 42
field: cancha, campo de fútbol U16, p. 39
fifteen: quince U19, p. 44
fifth: quinto U19, p. 45
fifty: cincuenta U19, p. 45
fig: higo U12, p. 31
file: archivar U14, p. 35
fill the tank: llenar el tanque U20, p. 47
film: película U15, p. 37
fire: incendio U22, p. 51
fire truck: camión de bomberos U22, p. 51
fireman: bombero U22, p. 51
first: primero U19, p. 45
    ~**course:** entrada, primer plato U13, p. 33
    ~**floor:** planta baja U7, p. 20
    ~**name:** nombre U22, p. 51
fish: pescado U11, p. 29; pescar U17, p. 41;

pez U23, p. 53
    ~**market:** pescadería U11, p. 29
fishing rod: caña de pescar U17, p. 41
fishmonger: pescadero U11, p. 29
fitting room: probador U4, p. 14
five: cinco U19, p. 44
flashlight: linterna U17, p. 41
flight: vuelo U21, p. 49
    ~**attendant:** auxiliar de vuelo, azafata U21, p. 48
float ring: flotador U17, p. 41
floor: piso U7, p. 21
florist: florería, floristería U10, p. 27
flour: harina U11, p. 29
flower: flor U10, p. 27
fly: volar U21, p. 48
foggy (to be ~): haber niebla U17, p. 40
folder: carpeta U14, p. 35
foot: pie U6, p. 19
football: fútbol americano U16, p. 38
forehead: frente U6, p. 19
forest: bosque U17, p. 40
fork: tenedor U13, p. 33
forty: cuarenta U19, p. 45
fountain: fuente U9, p. 25
four: cuatro U19, p. 44
fourteen: catorce U19, p. 44
fourth: cuarto U19, p. 45
fourth floor: tercer piso U7, p. 20
France: Francia U24, p. 56
freeway: autopista U20, p. 46
French: francés U24, p. 56
Friday: viernes U18, p. 43
friend: amigo U1, p. 8
friendly (to be ~): simpático (ser ~) U3, p. 12
frog: rana U23, p. 52
(in) front of (to be ~): enfrente, delante (estar ~) U7, p. 20
frozen foods: congelados U11, p. 28
fruit: fruta U11, p. 29
    ~**seller:** frutero U11, p. 29
    ~**shop:** frutería U11, p. 29
full (to be ~): lleno (estar ~) U3, p.13, U10, p. 27
funny (to be ~): gracioso (ser ~) U3, p. 12

---

g

garage: garaje U7, p. 21
garbage can: bote de basura, contenedor
    de basura U7, p. 21
garbanzo: garbanzo U12, p. 31
gardener: jardinero U5, p. 16
garlic: ajo U12, p. 30
gas: gasolina U20, p. 47
    ~**station:** gasolinera U20, p. 47
gate: puerta de embarque U21, p. 48
generous (to be ~): generoso (ser ~) U3, p. 12
German: alemán U24, p. 56
Germany: Alemania U24, p. 56
get a flat tire: pinchar una llanta U20, p. 47
    ~**bored:** aburrirse U15, p. 36
    ~**dark:** atardecer U18, p. 43
    ~**dressed:** vestirse U1, p. 9
    ~**light:** amanecer U18, p. 43
    ~**off a bus:** bajar del autobús U9, p. 25
    ~**on a bus:** subir al autobús U9, p. 25
    ~**up:** levantarse U1, p. 9
gift: regalo U1, p. 8

giraffe: jirafa U23, p. 53
girlfriend: novia U1, p. 8
glass: vaso U13, p. 33
   ~cabinet: vitrina U8, p. 23
gloves: guantes U4, p. 15
glove compartment: guantera U20, p. 47
glue: pegamento U14, p. 35
go by car: ir en auto U9, p. 25
   ~camping: acampar U17, p. 41
   ~canoeing: ir en canoa U17, p. 41
   ~fast: ir rápido U20, p. 46
   ~fishing: pescar U17, p. 41
   ~for a walk: pasear U15, p. 36
   ~hiking: hacer senderismo U17, p. 41
   ~horseback riding: montar a caballo U17, p. 41
   ~in: entrar U9, p. 24
   ~out: salir U9, p. 24
   ~scuba diving: hacer buceo, bucear U17, p. 41
   ~shopping: ir de compras U10, p. 26; hacer la compra, ir al supermercado U11, p. 28
   ~skiing: esquiar U17, p. 41
   ~straight: seguir derecho, seguir recto U9, p. 24
   ~to bed: acostarse U1, p. 9
   ~to the movies: ir al cine U15, p. 37
goal: arco, portería U16, p. 39
goalkeeper: arquero, portero U16, p. 39
goggles: gafas U16, p. 39
golf: golf U16, p. 38
   ~club: palo de golf U16, p. 38
good (to be ~): rico (estar ~), delicioso (estar ~) U13, p. 32
good-looking (to be ~): guapo (ser ~) U2, p. 10
granddaughter: nieta U1, p. 9
grandfather: abuelo U1, p. 9
grandmother: abuela U1, p. 9
grandparents: abuelos U1, p. 9
grandson: nieto U1, p. 9
grape: uva U12, p. 31
grass: pasto U17, p. 41
grass-eating (to be ~): herbívoro (ser ~) U23, p. 52
gray (to be ~): gris (ser ~) U19, p. 45
Greece: Grecia U24, p. 56
Greek: griego U24, p. 56
green (to be ~): verde (estar/ser ~) U12, p. 31, U19, p. 45
   ~bean: habichuela U12, p. 30
gross out: dar asco U3, p. 13
ground floor: planta baja U7, p. 20
Guatemala: Guatemala U24, p. 56
Guatemalan: guatemalteco U24, p. 56
guitar: guitarra U15, p. 37
gym: gimnasio U16, p. 39
gymnasium: gimnasio U16, p. 39

h

hair dryer: secador U8, p. 23
   ~salon: peluquería U10, p. 27
hairdresser: peluquero U10, p. 27
Haiti: Haití U24, p. 56
Haitian: haitiano U24, p. 56
hallway: pasillo U7, p. 21
ham: jamón U11, p. 29
hand: mano U6, p. 19
hanger: gancho, percha U4, p. 14
happy (to be ~): contento (estar ~), alegre (ser ~) U3, p. 12
hardworking (to be ~): trabajador (ser ~) U3, p. 12

hat: sombrero U4, p. 15
hate: odiar U3, p. 13
have a beard: tener barba U2, p. 11
   ~a beauty mark: tener un lunar U2, p. 11
   ~a business: tener una empresa U5, p. 17
   ~a cold: tener un resfriado U6, p. 18
   ~a degree: licenciado (ser ~) U5, p. 16
   ~a drink: tomar algo U15, p. 36
   ~a fever: tener fiebre U6, p. 18
   ~a good figure: tener buena figura U2, p. 10
   ~a headache: doler la cabeza U6, p. 18
   ~a mole: tener un lunar U2, p. 11
   ~a mustache: tener bigote U2, p. 11
   ~a ponytail: tener colitas U2, p. 11
   ~an afternoon snack: merendar U13, p. 32
   ~an appointment: tener una cita U14, p. 35
   ~bangs: llevar fleco, llevar flequillo U2, p. 11
   ~big eyes: tener los ojos grandes U2, p. 11
   ~black eyes: tener los ojos negros U2, p. 11
   ~blue eyes: tener los ojos azules U2, p. 11
   ~braids: tener trenzas U2, p. 11
   ~breakfast: desayunar U13, p. 32
   ~brown eyes: tener los ojos de color café, tener los ojos marrones U2, p. 11
   ~brown hair: tener pelo castaño U2, p. 11
   ~curly hair: tener el pelo rizado U2, p. 11
   ~dark eyes: tener los ojos oscuros U2, p. 11
   ~dinner: cenar U13, p. 32
   ~freckles: tener pecas U2, p. 11
   ~fun: divertirse U15, p. 36
   ~gray hair: tener canas U2, p. 11
   ~green eyes: tener los ojos verdes U2, p. 11
   ~light-colored eyes: tener ojos claros U2, p. 11
   ~long hair: tener el pelo largo U2, p. 11
   ~lunch: almorzar U13, p. 32
   ~red hair: pelirrojo (ser ~) U2, p. 11
   ~short hair: tener el pelo corto U2, p. 11
   ~small eyes: tener los ojos pequeños U2, p. 11
   ~straight hair: tener el pelo liso U2, p. 11
   ~supper: cenar U13, p. 32
   ~the flu: tener gripa, tener gripe U6, p. 18
   ~white hair: tener el pelo canoso U2, p. 11
hazelnut: avellana U12, p. 31
head: cabeza U6, p. 19
headlight: luz U20, p. 47
hearing impaired: persona con discapacidad auditiva, sordo (estar ~) U2, p. 10
heating: calefacción U7, p. 21
helmet: casco U16, p. 38
help: ayudar U22, p. 51
hen: gallina U23, p. 52
herbivorous (to be ~): herbívoro (ser ~) U23, p. 52
here (to be ~): acá (estar ~), aquí (estar ~) U7, p. 20
high-heeled shoes: zapatos de tacón U4, p. 15
highway: carretera U20, p. 46
hike: hacer senderismo U17, p. 41
Hindi: hindi U24, p. 56
hippopotamus: hipopótamo U23, p. 53
hire someone: contratar a alguien U14, p. 35
holiday: día feriado U18, p. 42
Honduran: hondureño U24, p. 56
Honduras: Honduras U24, p. 56
hood: capó U20, p. 47
horn: claxon, bocina U20, p. 47
horse: caballo U23, p. 52
hose: manguera U22, p. 51

hospital: hospital U6, p. 18
hot (to be ~): tener calor U3, p. 13; estar caliente U13, p. 32; hacer calor U17, p. 40
hotel: hotel U21, p. 49
hour: hora U18, p. 42
house: casa U7, p. 20
housewife: ama de casa U5, p. 17
hubcap: rin, llanta U20, p. 47
(a) hundred: cien U19, p. 45
hungry (to be ~): tener hambre U3, p. 13
husband: esposo U1, p. 8

i

ice cream: helado U13, p. 33
   ~cream parlor: heladería U10, p. 27
ill-mannered (to be ~): maleducado (ser ~) U3, p. 13
impatient (to be ~): impaciente (ser ~) U3, p. 13
index finger: dedo índice U6, p. 19
India: India U24, p. 56
Indian: indio U24, p. 56
Indian Ocean: Océano Índico U24, p. 56
inside (to be ~): adentro (estar ~) U7, p. 20
intelligent (to be ~): inteligente (ser ~) U3, p. 12
interpreter: intérprete U5, p. 16
interview: entrevista U14, p. 35
Ireland: Irlanda U24, p. 56
Irish: irlandés U24, p. 56
iron: plancha U8, p. 23
it´s exactly one o´clock: es la una en punto U18, p. 43
   ~five after four: son las cuatro y cinco U18, p. 43
   ~nine a.m.: son las nueve de la mañana U18, p. 43
   ~nine o´clock in the morning: son las nueve de la mañana U18, p. 43
   ~quarter after five: son las cinco y cuarto U18, p. 43
   ~quarter till seven: falta un cuarto para las siete, son las siete menos cuarto U18, p. 43
   ~six thirty: son las seis y media U18, p. 43
   ~ten o´clock at night: son las diez de la noche U18, p. 43
   ~ten of eight: faltan diez para las ocho, son las ocho menos diez U18, p. 43
   ~ten p.m.: son las diez de la noche U18, p. 43
Italian: italiano U24, p. 56
Italy: Italia U24, p. 56

j

jack: gato U20, p. 47
jacket: saco, chaqueta U4, p. 15
jam: mermelada U13, p. 33
January: enero U18, p. 42
Japan: Japón U24, p. 56
Japanese: japonés U24, p. 56
Javanese: javanés U24, p. 56
jealous (to be ~): envidioso (ser ~) U3, p. 13
jeans: *jeans*, (pantalones) vaqueros U4, p. 15
jewelry store: joyería U10, p. 27
journalist: periodista U5, p. 16
judge: juez U5, p. 16
juice: jugo, zumo U11, p. 29
July: julio U18, p. 42
jump: saltar U16, p. 39
June: junio U18, p. 42

k

keyboard: teclado U14, p. 35
kilo: kilo U11, p. 29
kind (to be ~): amable (ser ~) U3, p. 12
kiosk: puesto de periódicos U10, p. 27
kiss: besar U3, p. 13
kitchen: cocina U8, p. 22
kite: papalote, cometa U15, p. 37
kiwi: kiwi U12, p. 31
knee: rodilla U6, p. 19
knife: cuchillo U13, p. 33
knit: tejer U15, p. 36
Korean: coreano U24, p. 56

l

lab: laboratorio U5, p. 17
laboratory: laboratorio U5, p. 17
lake: lago U17, p. 41
lamp: lámpara U8, p. 23
land: aterrizar U21, p. 48
lane: carril U20, p. 46
laptop computer: *laptop*, computadora portátil U14, p. 35
large (to be ~): grande (estar/ser ~) U19, p. 44
last name: apellido U22, p. 51
laugh: reír U3, p. 13
laundromat: lavandería U10, p. 27
law firm: bufete U5, p. 17
lawyer: abogado U5, p. 16
lazy (to be ~): flojo (ser ~), vago (ser ~) U3, p. 12
leave: salir U9, p. 24
   ~a message: dejar un recado U14, p. 34
   ~a tip: dejar una propina U13, p. 32
leek: puerro U12, p. 30
leg: pierna U6, p. 19; pata U23, p. 53
lemon: limón U12, p. 31
lentil: lenteja U12, p. 31
letter: carta U22, p. 51
lettuce: lechuga U12, p. 30
library: biblioteca U9, p. 24
license plate: placa, matrícula U20, p. 47
life vest: chaleco salvavidas U17, p. 41
lifeguard: salvavidas U17, p. 41
like: gustar U3, p. 13
lime: lima U12, p. 31
lion: león U23, p. 52
lips: labios U6, p. 19
liquid soap: gel U8, p. 23
listen music: escuchar música U15, p. 37
liter: litro U11, p. 29
little (to be ~): pequeño (estar/ser ~) U19, p. 44
   ~finger: dedo meñique U6, p. 19
living room: sala, salón U8, p. 22
loaf of bread: barra de pan U11, p. 29
long (to be ~): largo (estar ~) U4, p. 14
look at a map: mirar un mapa U21, p. 49
   ~like someone: parecerse a alguien U2, p. 10
loose (to be ~): ancho (estar ~) U4, p. 14
lose: perder U16, p. 38
love: querer U3, p. 13
(in) love (to be ~): enamorado (estar ~) U3, p. 13
luggage: equipaje U21, p. 49
lying down (to be ~): acostado (estar ~) U6, p. 19

m

mailbox: buzón U9, p. 25
mailman: cartero U22, p. 50
make a reservation: hacer una reserva, hacer una reservación U21, p. 49
 ~ photocopies: fotocopiar, hacer fotocopias U14, p. 35
 ~ the bed: tender la cama U8, p. 22
man: hombre U2, p. 10
manager: gerente, director U14, p. 34
mandarin orange: mandarina U12, p. 31
map: mapa U21, p. 48
March: marzo U18, p. 42
married (to be ~): casado (estar/ser ~) U1, p. 8
May: mayo U18, p. 42
mayor: alcalde U5, p. 16
meat: carne U11, p. 29
meat-eating: carnívoro (ser ~) U23, p. 52
mechanic: mecánico U5, p. 17
medicine: medicamento U6, p. 18
meet: reunirse U14, p. 34
meet (up with): quedar U15, p. 36
meeting: reunión U14, p. 34
melon: melón U12, p. 31
merry-go-round: carrusel U15, p. 37
messenger: mensajero U22, p. 50
messy (to be ~): desordenado (ser ~) U3, p. 13
mew: maullar U23, p. 52
Mexican: mexicano U24, p. 56
Mexico: México U24, p. 56
microwave: microondas U8, p. 23
(in the) middle (to be~): (en el) centro (estar ~) U7, p. 20
middle finger: dedo corazón U6, p. 19
(at) midnight: (a) medianoche U18, p. 43
milk: leche U11, p. 29
(at) million: (un) millón U19, p. 45
minute: minuto U18, p. 43
mirror: espejo U8, p. 22
mischievous (to be ~): travieso (ser ~) U3, p. 12
miss: echar de menos, extrañar U3, p. 13
 ~ the plane: perder el avión U21, p. 48
molar: muela U6, p. 19
Monday: lunes U18, p. 43
money: dinero U22, p. 50
monkey: mono U23, p. 53
month: mes U18, p. 42
moo: mugir U23, p. 52
moon: luna U17, p. 40
(in the) morning: en la mañana, por la mañana U18, p. 43
Moroccan: marroquí U24, p. 56
Morocco: Marruecos U24, p. 56
mosquito: mosquito U23, p. 53
mother: madre, mamá U1, p. 9
mother-in-law: suegra U1, p. 8
motorcycle: moto U9, p. 25
mountain: montaña U17, p. 40
mouse: ratón U14, p. 35
mouth: boca U6, p. 19
move: mudarse U7, p. 21
movie theater: cine U15, p. 37
museum: museo U15, p. 37
musician: músico U15, p. 37

n

napkin: servilleta U13, p. 32
near (to be ~): cerca (estar ~) U7, p. 20
neat (to be ~): ordenado (ser ~) U3, p. 13
neck: cuello U6, p. 19
necklace: collar U4, p. 15
neigh: relinchar U23, p. 52
neighbor: vecino U7, p. 21
neighborhood: barrio U9, p. 24
nephew: sobrino U1, p. 8
nervous (to be ~): nervioso (estar ~) U3, p. 12
net: red U16, p. 39
(the) Netherlands (Holland): Países Bajos (Holanda) U24, p. 56
new (to be ~): nuevo (estar/ser ~) U19, p. 44
New Year´s Day: Año Nuevo U18, p. 42
newspaper kiosk: quiosco U10, p. 27
next to (to be ~): (al) lado (estar ~) U7, p. 20
Nicaragua: Nicaragua U24, p. 56
Nicaraguan: nicaragüense U24, p. 56
nice (to be ~): amable (ser ~) U3, p. 12; lindo (ser ~), bonito (ser ~) U4, p. 14
niece: sobrina U1, p. 8
(at) night: en la noche, por la noche U18, p. 43
nightstand: mesita de noche U8, p. 23
nine: nueve U19, p. 44
nineteen: diecinueve U19, p. 45
ninety: noventa U19, p. 45
ninth: noveno U19, p. 45
(at) noon: (al) mediodía U18, p. 43
North: Norte U24, p. 56
 ~ America: América del Norte U24, p. 56
Norway: Noruega U24, p. 56
Norwegian: noruego U24, p. 56
nose: nariz U6, p. 19
notebook: cuaderno U14, p. 35
notice board: tablero de anuncios U14, p. 34
November: noviembre U18, p. 42
nurse: enfermero U6, p. 18

o

obedient (to be ~): obediente (ser ~) U3, p. 12
Oceania: Oceanía U24, p. 56
October: octubre U18, p. 42
octopus: pulpo U23, p. 53
office: despacho U8, p. 22, U14, p. 34
oil: aceite U13, p. 33
old (to be ~): mayor (ser ~) U2, p. 10; viejo (estar/ser ~) U19, p. 44
 ~ man: anciano, viejito U2, p. 10
older (to be ~): mayor (ser ~) U2, p. 10; viejo (estar/ser ~) U19, p. 44
one: uno U19, p. 44
onion: cebolla U12, p. 30
only child: hijo único U1, p. 8
open (to be ~): abierto (estar ~) U7, p. 21
 ~ a letter: abrir una carta U22, p. 50
optician: óptica U10, p. 27
optimistic (to be ~): optimista (ser ~) U3, p. 12
orange: naranja U12, p. 31
 ~ (to be ~): anaranjado (ser ~) U19, p. 45

orchestra: orquesta U15, p. 37
order: pedir U13, p. 32
outside (to be ~): afuera (estar ~) U7, p. 20
outskirts: afueras U9, p. 24
oven: horno U8, p. 23
overcast (to be ~): nublado (estar ~) U17, p. 40
overpass: puente U20, p. 46
over there (to be ~): allá (estar ~)

p

Pacific Ocean: Océano Pacífico U24, p. 56
pack (suitcases, bags): hacer las maletas U21, p. 49
package: paquete U11, p. 29, U22, p. 50
paint: pintar U15, p. 36
painter: pintor U5, p. 17
painting: cuadro U15, p. 37
pajamas: piyama, pijama U4, p. 15
Panama: Panamá U24, p. 56
Panamanian: panameño U24, p. 56
panties: calzones, bragas U4, p. 15
pants: pantalón, pantalones U4, p. 15
paper clip: sujetapapeles, clip U14, p. 35
Paraguay: Paraguay U24, p. 56
Paraguayan: paraguayo U24, p. 56
parents: padres U1, p. 9
park: parque U9, p. 24; estacionarse U20, p. 46
parking lot: estacionamiento U9, p. 25
parrot: loro U23, p. 53
parsley: perejil U12, p. 30
pass: adelantar, pasar U20, p. 46
  ~ (the ball): pasar la pelota U16, p. 39
passbook: cartilla U22, p. 51
passenger: pasajero U21, p. 48
passport: pasaporte U21, p. 48
pasta: pasta U11, p. 29
patient: paciente U6, p. 18
patrol car: patrulla U22, p. 51
pay (in) cash: pagar en efectivo U11, p. 28
  ~ for someone: invitar U15, p. 36
  ~ with a credit card: pagar con tarjeta U11, p. 28
pea: arveja U12, p. 30
peach: durazno U12, p. 31
peanut: cacahuate, maní U12, p. 31
pear: pera U12, p. 31
pedestrian: peatón U9, p. 25
pen: bolígrafo U14, p. 35
pencil: lápiz U14, p. 35
penguin: pingüino U23, p. 53
penthouse: *penthouse* U7, p. 20
pepper: pimienta U13, p. 33
Peru: Perú U24, p. 56
Peruvian: peruano U24, p. 56
pessimistic (to be ~): pesimista (ser ~) U3, p. 12
pharmacist: farmacéutico U10, p. 27
pharmacy: farmacia U10, p. 27
photocopier: fotocopiadora U14, p. 35
photocopy: fotocopiar, hacer fotocopias U14, p. 35
photographer: fotógrafo U5, p. 16
physically challenged: persona con discapacidad física U2, p. 10
piano: piano U15, p. 37
pick up the luggage: recoger el equipaje U21, p. 48
pig: cerdo U23, p. 52
pillow: almohada U8, p. 23
pilot: piloto U21, p. 48

pine nut: piñón U12, p. 31
pineapple: piña U12, p. 31
pistachio: pistache, pistacho U12, p. 31
pitcher: jarra U13, p. 33
plain (to be ~): liso (ser ~) U4, p. 14
plant: planta U10, p. 27
plate (dinner): plato llano U13, p. 33
platform: andén U9, p. 25
play: obra de teatro U15, p. 37
  ~ an instrument: tocar un instrumento U15, p. 37
  ~ cards: jugar a las cartas U15, p. 36
  ~ chess: jugar al ajedrez U15, p. 36
  ~ hide-and-go-seek: jugar a las escondidas, jugar al escondite U15, p. 36
  ~ soccer: jugar al fútbol U16, p. 39
player: jugador U16, p. 39
plumber: plomero U5, p. 17
poisonous (to be ~): venenoso (ser ~) U23, p. 52
Poland: Polonia U24, p. 56
police officer: policía U22, p. 51
  ~ station: comisaría U22, p. 51
Polish: polaco U24, p. 56
polite (to be ~): educado (ser ~) U3, p. 13
polka-dotted (to be ~): (a) lunares (ser ~) U4, p. 14
pork: cerdo U11, p. 29
Portuguese: portugués U24, p. 56
post: repartir el correo U22, p. 50
  ~ office: oficina de correos U22, p. 50
postcard: postal U22, p. 50
potato: papa U12, p. 30
pregnant (to be ~): embarazada (estar ~) U2, p. 10
prescription: receta U6, p. 18
pretty (to be ~): lindo (ser ~), bonito (ser ~) U4, p. 14
price: precio U10, p. 26
priest: sacerdote U5, p. 16
print: imprimir U14, p. 34
printer: impresora U14, p. 34
priority mail: correo urgente U22, p. 50
professor: profesor U5, p. 17
proud (to be ~): orgulloso (estar ~) U3, p. 13
psychologist: psicólogo U5, p. 17
psychologist's office: consultorio, consulta del psicólogo U5, p. 17
pumpkin: calabaza U12, p. 30
pupil: pupila U6, p. 19
purse: bolsa, bolso U4, p. 15
push: empujar U20, p. 47
  ~ air in the tire: inflar la llanta U20, p. 47
  ~ on sunscreen: ponerse bloqueador solar U17, p. 41
  ~ on: ponerse U4, p. 14
  ~ out a fire: apagar un incendio U22, p. 51

r

rabbit: conejo U23, p. 53
racket: raqueta U16, p. 39
radiator: radiador U20, p. 47
radish: rábano U12, p. 30
rain: llover U17, p. 40
raspberry: frambuesa U12, p. 31
read a novel: leer una novela U15, p. 36
  ~ the newspaper: leer el periódico U1, p. 9
receipt: recibo, ticket U10, p. 26
receive a letter: recibir una carta U22, p. 50
reception: recepción U21, p. 49
  ~ desk: recepción U14, p. 34

receptionist: recepcionista U21, p. 49
record store: tienda de discos U10, p. 27
red (to be ~): rojo (ser ~) U19, p. 45
referee: árbitro U16, p. 39
refrigerator: nevera, refrigerador U8, p. 23
rent: alquilar U7, p. 21
rest: descansar U16, p. 38
résumé: currículum U14, p. 35
retired (to be ~): jubilado (estar ~) U5, p. 16
return: devolver U10, p. 26
rice: arroz U11, p. 29
ride a bike: montar en bicicleta U16, p. 38
   ~ horses: montar a caballo U17, p. 41
ring: sortija, anillo U4, p. 15
   ~ finger: dedo anular U6, p. 19
ripe (to be ~): maduro (estar ~) U12, p. 31
river: río U17, p. 41
roar: rugir U23, p. 52
rob (a person or place): robar U22, p. 50
roller-skate: patinar U15, p. 36
roof: techo, tejado U7, p. 21
room service: servicio de habitaciones U21, p. 49
rotten (to be ~): podrido (estar ~) U12, p. 31
round (to be ~): redondo (ser ~) U19, p. 44
rucksack: mochila U21, p. 49
rude (to be ~): maleducado (ser ~) U3, p. 13
rug: alfombra U8, p. 23
run: correr U16, p. 38
runway: pista de aterrizaje U21, p. 48
Russia: Rusia U24, p. 56
Russian: ruso U24, p. 56

S

sad (to be ~): triste (estar ~) U3, p. 12
sailboat: barco de vela U17, p. 41
salad: ensalada U13, p. 33
(on) sale (to be ~): (de) oferta (estar ~) U10, p. 27
sales: ofertas, rebajas U10, p. 26
   ~ representative: vendedor U5, p. 16
salt: sal U13, p. 33
Salvadorian: salvadoreño U24, p. 56
sand: arena U17, p. 41
sandals: sandalias U4, p. 15
sandwich: sándwich U13, p. 33
Saturday: sábado U18, p. 43
say good-bye: despedirse U21, p. 48
scarf: bufanda U4, p. 15; pañoleta, pañuelo U4, p. 15
scenery: escenografía, decorado U15, p. 37
school: escuela U9, p. 24
scientist: científico U5, p. 17
score a goal: meter un gol U16, p. 39
scoreboard: marcador U16, p. 39
Scotch tape®: cinta adhesiva U14, p. 35
screen: pantalla U14, p. 35
sculpture: escultura U15, p. 37
sea: mar U17, p. 41
seal: foca U23, p. 53
   ~ a letter: cerrar una carta U22, p. 50
seat: butaca U15, p. 37; asiento U20, p. 47
   ~ belt: cinturón de seguridad U20, p. 47
seated (to be ~): sentado (estar ~) U6, p. 19
second: segundo U18, p. 43, U19, p. 45
   ~ course: plato fuerte, segundo plato U13, p. 33
   ~ floor: primer piso U7, p. 20
secretary: secretario U14, p. 34

security guard: guardia de seguridad U22, p. 51
see an exhibition: visitar una exposición U15, p. 37
seesaw: subibaja, balancín U15, p. 37
selfish (to be ~): egoísta (ser ~) U3, p. 12
sell: vender U7, p. 21
send a fax: enviar un fax U14, p. 34
   ~ a package: enviar un paquete U22, p. 50
sender: remitente U22, p. 51
September: septiembre U18, p. 42
serious (to be ~): serio (ser ~) U3, p. 12
service station: área de servicio U20, p. 46
seven: siete U19, p. 44
seventeen: diecisiete U19, p. 45
seventh: séptimo U19, p. 45
seventy: setenta U19, p. 45
sewer: alcantarilla U9, p. 25
shampoo: champú U8, p. 23
shark: tiburón U23, p. 53
shave: afeitarse U1, p. 9
sheep: oveja U23, p. 52
sheet: hoja U14, p. 35
sheets: sábanas U8, p. 23
shellfish: marisco U11, p. 29
shirt: camisa U4, p. 15
shoes: zapatos U4, p. 15
shoe store: zapatería U10, p. 27
shopping cart: carro U11, p. 28
   ~ center: centro comercial U10, p. 26
   ~ list: lista del supermercado, lista
      de la compra U11, p. 28
   ~ mall: centro comercial U10, p. 26
shore: orilla U17, p. 41
short (to be ~): bajo (ser ~) U2, p. 10; corto (estar ~)
      U4, p. 14
shorts: pantalón corto U16, p. 38
shoulder: hombro U6, p. 19; acotamiento,
      arcén U20, p. 46
shower: ducha U8, p. 23
   ~ gel: gel U8, p. 23
shredder: trituradora de papel U14, p. 35
shy (to be ~): tímido (ser ~) U3, p. 12
sick (to be ~): enfermo (estar ~) U6, p. 18
sidewalk: acera U9, p. 24
sight impaired: persona con discapacidad visual,
      ciego (estar ~) U2, p. 10
sign: firmar U14, p. 34
sing: cantar U15, p. 37
singer: cantante U15, p. 37
single (to be ~): soltero (estar/ser ~) U1, p. 8
   ~ room: habitación individual U21, p. 49
sink: fregadero U8, p. 23; lavamanos,
      lavabo U8, p. 23
sister: hermana U1, p. 9
sitting (to be ~): sentado (estar ~) U6, p. 19
six: seis U19, p. 44
sixteen: dieciséis U19, p. 45
sixth: sexto U19, p. 45
sixty: sesenta U19, p. 45
size: talla U4, p. 14
skateboard: patineta U15, p. 36
ski: esquiar U17, p. 41
skip: saltar a la cuerda U15, p. 37
skirt: falda U4, p. 15
sky: cielo U17, p. 40
skyscraper: rascacielos U9, p. 24
sleep: dormir U1, p. 9

sleeping bag: saco de dormir U17, p. 41
sleepy (to be ~): tener sueño U3, p. 13
slide: tobogán U15, p. 37
slippers: pantuflas U4, p. 15
small (to be ~): pequeño (estar/ser ~) U19, p. 44
snail: caracol U23, p. 53
snake: serpiente U23, p. 53
sneakers: zapatillas de tenis U16, p. 38
sneeze: estornudar U6, p. 18
snout: hocico U23, p. 53
snow: nevar U17, p. 40
snowman: muñeco de nieve U17, p. 41
soap: jabón U8, p. 23
soccer: fútbol U16, p. 38
sociable (to be ~): sociable (ser ~) U3, p. 12
socket: enchufe U8, p. 22
socks: calcetines U4, p. 15
sofa: sofá U8, p. 23
soldier: soldado U5, p. 16
son: hijo U1, p. 9
son-in-law: yerno U1, p. 8
soup: sopa U13, p. 33
  ~ bowl: plato hondo U13, p. 33
  ~ tureen: sopera U13, p. 33
South: Sur U24, p. 56
  ~ Africa: Suráfrica U24, p. 56
  ~ African: surafricano U24, p. 56
  ~ America: América del Sur U24, p. 56
Spain: España U24, p. 56
Spanish: español U24, p. 56
speed: ir rápido U20, p. 46
spinach: espinaca U12, p. 30
sponge: esponja U8, p. 23
spoon: cuchara U13, p. 33
spring: primavera U17, p. 40
square: plaza U9, p. 24
  ~ (to be ~): cuadrado (ser ~) U19, p. 44
stable: establo U17, p. 41
stage: escenario U15, p. 37
stairway: escalera U7, p. 21
stamp: timbre, sello U22, p. 51
stand in a line: hacer cola U11, p. 28
standing (to be ~): (de) pie (estar ~) U6, p. 19
stapler: engrapadora, grapadora U14, p. 35
star: estrella U17, p. 40
starfish: estrella de mar U23, p. 53
start (up): arrancar U20, p. 46
statement: estado de cuenta, extracto U22, p. 51
stationery store: papelería U10, p. 27
steak with potatoes: bistec con papas U13, p. 33
steal (something): robar U22, p. 50
steering wheel: volante U20, p. 47
stick shift: caja de velocidades, caja de cambios U20, p. 47
sting: picar U23, p. 52
stockings: medias U4, p. 15
stomach: estómago U6, p. 19
stop: frenar U20, p. 46
stormy (to be ~): haber tormenta U17, p. 40
straw: pajita U13, p. 33
strawberry: fresa U12, p. 31
street: calle U9, p. 24
  ~ cleaner: barrendero U5, p. 16
streetlight: farol, farola U9, p. 25
striped (to be ~): (a) rayas (ser ~) U4, p. 14
strong (to be ~): fuerte (ser ~) U2, p. 10

student: estudiante U5, p. 17
studio apartment: estudio U7, p. 20
study: estudiar U5, p. 17
subway station: estación de metro U9, p. 25
sugar bowl: azucarera, azucarero U13, p. 33
suit: traje U4, p. 15
suitcase: maleta U21, p. 49
summer: verano U17, p. 40
sun: sol U17, p. 40
sunbathe: tomar el sol U17, p. 41
Sunday: domingo U18, p. 43
sunglasses: lentes de sol, gafas de sol U4, p. 15
surf: hacer surf U17, p. 41
  ~ (the Internet, the Web): navegar (por Internet, la red) U14, p. 35
surgeon: cirujano U6, p. 18
surprised (to be ~): sorprendido (estar ~) U3, p. 13
sweater: suéter U4, p. 15
sweatsuit: sudadera U16, p. 38
Sweden: Suecia U24, p. 56
Swedish: sueco U24, p. 56
swim: nadar U16, p. 39
  ~ (the) backstroke: nadar estilo espalda U16, p. 39
  ~ (the) breaststroke: nadar estilo pecho U16, p. 39
  ~ butterfly: nadar estilo mariposa U16, p. 39
  ~ cap: gorro U16, p. 39
  ~ the crawl: nadar estilo crol U16, p. 39
swimming: natación U16, p. 38
  ~ pool: piscina U16, p. 39
swimsuit: traje de baño U4, p. 15
swing: columpio U15, p. 37
Swiss: suizo U24, p. 56
  ~ chard: acelga U12, p. 30
Switzerland: Suiza U24, p. 56
syringe: jeringa, jeringuilla U6, p. 18

t

table: mesa U8, p. 23
tablecloth: mantel U13, p. 32
tag: etiqueta U10, p. 26
tail: cola U21, p. 49, U23, p. 53
talk: hablar U1, p. 9
take a bath: bañarse U1, p. 9
  ~ a shower: ducharse U1, p. 9
  ~ off: quitarse U4, p. 14; despegar U21, p. 48
  ~ on: contratar a alguien U14, p. 35
  ~ out money: sacar dinero U22, p. 51
  ~ photos: tomar fotografías U15, p. 36
  ~ the train: tomar el tren U9, p. 25
talk on the phone: llamar por teléfono U14, p. 34
talkative (to be ~): hablador (ser ~) U3, p. 13
tall (to be ~): alto (ser ~) U2, p. 10
tame (to be ~): manso (ser ~) U23, p. 52
tan (to be ~): bronceado (estar ~) U2, p. 11
tangerine: mandarina U12, p. 31
tape: cinta adhesiva U14, p. 35
taxi: taxi U9, p. 25
  ~ driver: taxista U9, p. 25
  ~ stand: parada de taxis U9, p. 25
tea: té U13, p. 33
teacher: profesor U5, p. 17
team: equipo U16, p. 39
teapot: tetera U13, p. 33
teaspoon: cucharita U13, p. 33